BOMB CANADA

BOMB CANADA

AND OTHER UNKIND REMARKS

IN THE AMERICAN MEDIA

CHANTAL ALLAN

AU PRESS

Global Peace Studies series

© 2009 Chantal Allan
Second printing 2010

Published by AU Press, Athabasca University
1200, 10011 - 109 Street
AU PRESS   Edmonton, AB T5J 3S8

A volume in the Global Peace Studies series, edited by George Melnyk
ISSN 1921-4022 Global Peace Studies series (Print)
ISSN 1921-4030 Global Peace Studies series (Online)

Library and Archives Canada Cataloguing in Publication

Allan, Chantal, 1979-
    Bomb Canada : and other unkind remarks in the American media /
    Chantal Allan.

(Global peace studies)
Includes bibliographical references.
ISBN 978-1-897425-49-7
Also available in PDF format ISBN 978-1-897425-50-3

    1. Canada - Relations - United States. 2. United States - Relations - Canada.
I. Title. II. Series: Global peace studies

FC249.A45 2009   303.48'271073   C2009-903680-0

Printed and bound in Canada by Marquis Book Printing
Cover design by Rod Michalchuk
Book layout and design by Helen Adhikari

AU Press gratefully acknowledges the support of the
Alberta Foundation for the Arts.

For Norm and Solange

★★★ CONTENTS ★★★

★★★ PREFACE ★★★

The article is wrinkled and aging. The photograph of U.S. Ambassador David Wilkins in an Ottawa Senators jersey smudged and faded. I cut out the story in December 2005 when I was home in Winnipeg for the Christmas holidays. I had moved to Los Angeles a few months earlier so the picture of Wilkins in the *Winnipeg Free Press* with the headline "We're slow and 'stalking' America, says TV pundit" caught my attention. MSNBC's Tucker Carlson had just made his infamous "Canada is your retarded cousin" comment and the Canadian press was indignant at this latest verbal slight as well as some other equally provocative Canada-bashing remarks. As a journalist and now an incognito Canadian, I was intrigued. Why were American commentators taking aim at Canada? And how did this compare to what has been said by the American media in the past? So began the process of sifting through thousands of newspaper and magazine articles, trolling the Internet for anti-Canadian blog postings and keeping track of television comments. In essence, it is a project with no finite end.

I want to thank all those who contributed in even the smallest way to this book. To my family and friends who offered encouragement and passed along tidbits they heard or read in the news; to those who always picked up the phone when I called and helped me navigate writer's block; to my husband Ryan who rallied behind me, providing steadfast support and suffering through more than his fair share of burned leftovers.

None of this would have been possible if not for Bryce Nelson. Thank you, Bryce for giving me freedom to write that first piece and urging me on by saying I could do better. My deepest regards and thanks as well to Patrick James who unknowingly picked up where Bryce left off. Your advice, enthusiasm, and confidence in this body of work have been truly appreciated.

Without the opportunities you gave me, the book would never have been written.

I'm also grateful to Janice Dickin for her early support of this project as well as Walter Hildebrandt, Erna Dominey, Brenda Hennig, Carol Woo, and Ruth Bradley-St-Cyr for their guidance and insights. To the anonymous assessors, I'm grateful for your frank criticisms and suggestions.

This book is a compilation of original news reports, and as such, some facts may be regarded as inaccurate in hindsight. Finally, while reading these pages may you, the reader, gain greater appreciation and understanding of the complexities that define the relationship between Canada and the United States.

Chantal Nikkel Allan
July 2009
Los Angeles, California

Canadianism:
the state of being Canadian *(Oxford Canadian Dictionary)*

+

anti:
opposed to; against *(Oxford Canadian Dictionary)*

=

anti-Canadianism:
opposed to the state of being Canadian *(Bomb Canada)*

Anti-Canadianism, anti-Canuckism — call it what you will, it's hard to find a definition in contemporary dictionaries for the act of bashing Canada. Surprising? Not really. While scholars in Canada and the United States have studied anti-Americanism in depth, anti-Canadianism has largely been neglected, left on the bench you could say as America-bashing comments take centre ice. Yet that doesn't mean it's irrelevant.

The relationship between Canada and the United States has been compared to that of siblings — or jilted lovers inexplicably drawn back together over, and over, and over again. It's a complex history that entwines periods of tension and reconciliation. In 1776, almost a century before Canada's Dominion Day celebrations, the Thirteen Colonies issued a Declaration of Independence and invited the four other British colonies in North America — Quebec, Nova Scotia, Prince Edward Island, and Newfoundland — to join a revolt against Britain. These colonies, much to the surprise of the fledgling United States, refused, in essence placing loyalty to the monarchy over that of a republic. The War of 1812 further cemented Canadian ties to the British. Simmering trade and sovereignty disputes erupted in violence again when the United States declared war on Britain and launched pre-emptive attacks against Upper and Lower Canada. Perplexed by the British colonies' allegiance to the Crown, Americans were convinced the colonists desired to be liberated from Britain too. But the Canadian and Native peoples fought alongside British forces, repelling the American invasions and in the process burning the White House in Washington, D.C.

Why mention these events from centuries past? Because they are the foundation upon which anti-Canadianism has been built. The roots of negativity towards Canada unavoidably trace back to the United States' turbulent relationship with Britain. And while Canada has obtained full independence from Mother England, the country's ideals and values continue to reflect more closely those from across the sea than those of the republic to the south.

Mostly, the American–Canadian relationship has been one of stability, particularly since the mid-twentieth century. Though they had contingency plans for war with the other — Canada devised "Defence Scheme No. 1" in 1921 and the United States drew up "War Plan Red" in the early 1930s — the economic, the cultural, and increasingly, the defence ties have become so tightly woven that unbraiding them would threaten the security and prosperity of both nations.

Still, understanding the shared but ultimately different destinies of the two countries helps explain why there's a nagging sense of mistrust or anxiety that has coloured cross-border relations every so often since the United States gained its independence. Overt gestures by the American government for increased co-operation have been denounced as concealed aspirations of annexation from the Canadian side. And when the Canadian government exerts its sovereignty against certain U.S. policies, American reaction has been similar to that of being betrayed by a best friend. In those times of tension, whether it be Canada's creation as a Dominion, the failed 1911 Reciprocity Treaty, the Cuban missile crisis, Vietnam, the Trudeau years, the war in Iraq or terrorism, the American media has been scrupulously — some would argue erroneously — recording the events and ideas of the moment.

Modern-day journalism traces back to the hurly-burly days of the penny press, which emerged in the 1830s. From those humble, often-colourful beginnings were born newspapers that would gain national prominence, including the *Chicago Tribune* founded in 1847 and the *New York Times* in 1851. Within four and a half decades, printing presses were churning out the *Washington Post*, the *Los Angeles Times*, and the *Wall Street Journal*. Into the twentieth century, the term "media" broadened as the number of national magazines increased and technological advances allowed the news to be presented in radio and television formats. Now in the twenty-first century, blogs and online media outlets have ushered in a new era of journalism, one that is more transparent and immediate than ever before.

Of course, in the midst of this information overload, it would be a monumental task to compile Canadian coverage from every newspaper, magazine, and broadcast outlet in the United States. So from hundreds, it has been whittled down to a select few. While blog and TV comments are important and mentioned in later chapters, national newspapers are prominently featured because they have reported on Canada for a period stretching over three centuries. In particular, the *New York Times*, *Chicago Tribune*, *Los Angeles Times*, *Washington Post*, and *Wall Street Journal* have been chosen because they have stood the test of time, not only surviving as competing papers folded but also growing in national eminence. As leading media outlets in the United States, these newspapers have reached a broad audience, influencing members of Congress, local policy makers, and popular opinion.

"Journalism is the first rough draft of history." So goes the oft-quoted cliché credited to *Washington Post* publisher Philip Graham. Spanning more than 140 years — from the creation of the Dominion of Canada in 1867 to terrorism in the new millennium — here's an initial, informative, and often humorous look at anti-Canadianism from the south side of the 49th parallel. This is the "uncut" version of Canada–U.S. relations. Before the history books were written, turn the page to hear what the press was saying.

CHAPTER 1

THE FIRST FIVE YEARS

1867–1872

He shall have Dominion also from sea to sea, and from the river unto the ends of the earth. ~ *Psalm 72:8*[1]

I fear that I have not got much to say about Canada, not having seen much; what I got by going to Canada was a cold. ~ *Henry David Thoreau, 1866*

For Americans living south of Britain's colonies in North America, life on the other side of the border appeared undeniably dreary in the mid-nineteenth century. Thoreau's impressions of Canada seemed unchanged from the words penned by Voltaire a century before – "*quelques arpents de neige*"– was his dismissive remark, "a few acres of snow." Then news reached the United States that Canada was gaining quasi-independence from Britain through the British North America Act and would no longer be regarded as a colony but a country within the British Empire.

At the *Chicago Tribune* and the *New York Times*,[2] attention focused on Canada's potential as a nation. With its snow and ice, and its scattered population one-tenth the size of the growing American states, could it survive? Even more, dare it be said the emerging "Kingdom of Canada" could one day be a threat? "Nonsense!" exclaimed the *Chicago Tribune*. On the evening of 27 February 1867, Representative Henry J. Raymond, founder and editor of the *New York Times*, tried to bring a resolution before Congress declaring that the establishment of Canada as a constitutional monarchy "cannot be regarded otherwise than as being hostile to the peace, and menacing to the safety of this Republic."[3]

"The 'powerful monarchy' of Canada!" responded the *Tribune* sarcastically. "The idea that the United States has any reason to fear Canada, is too ridiculous to find lodgment in any sensible man's brain, and we must conclude that Mr. Raymond's resolution was pure buncombe."[4]

But talk of the new country being named the "Kingdom of Canada" puzzled those at the *Tribune*, especially when a dispatch from Montreal announced that Queen Victoria's son, 17-year-old Prince Arthur, would be Canada's first governor general:

> Whether this position be temporary, or whether it contemplates the ultimate foundation of a royal dynasty on this Continent, is, of course, unknown. It is not reasonable to suppose that a Prince of the royal family – a son of the reigning Queen, and brother to the heir apparent – will accept, with any view to permanency, the mere Governorship of the Canadian Provinces.[5]

Britain of course, was a powerful monarchy at the time. But the *Tribune* predicted that any new monarchy in the British colonies would fail. "Canada, even in her present semi-democratic government, is avoided by all the enterprise, and labor, and capital, of the world," it wrote. "The result is that her stagnant and impecunious condition is painful and distressing to behold."[6]

At the *New York Times*, a correspondent in Toronto sent back reports assessing Canada's future. As often seen in the early bustling days of the press, the reporter remains anonymous. Canada, the unnamed journalist said, would flourish as a constitutional monarchy, but the new nation could stumble from a lack of funds. The creation of the Dominion – as it was decided Canada would be called –"brings us to a new era in the history of British North America, but the cost will be greater, and each Province by having the power to manage its own local affairs will find the expense increased beyond its expectation," the correspondent wrote. "The General Government being more extensive, will require a greater revenue without the corresponding means of raising it."[7]

Among its new expenditures, the Canadian government would have to maintain a military as Britain would soon be withdrawing a majority of its troops. Without the British, the situation appeared bleak. The *New York Times* noted that even "the most enthusiastic members of the Confederate party are obliged to confess that the local force to-day, unsupported by the British regulars, would form a poor nucleus for a Provincial Union army in case of war."[8]

Further, the paper argued, the hoped-for number of recruits needed to build an army of any respectable strength didn't add up. A troop size of 335,000 through conscription or forced limited terms of service was discussed with Nova Scotia responsible for providing 30,000 soldiers, New Brunswick — 25,000, Lower Canada (Quebec) — 120,000, and Upper Canada (Ontario) — 160,000. But as the *Times* pointed out, these numbers would mean conscripting 10 percent of the entire population in the colonies including men, women, and children, or enlisting nearly half of the men under fifty years of age. Canada, wrote the paper, was deluding itself into thinking that a population of three and a half million could properly defend itself. It would be lucky to have an army twenty thousand strong. The solution, the *Times* said, was simple: politicians needed to "cultivate the friendship and win the good-will of the Government and people of the United States. That will stand it in better stead than an army — large or small — organized by visionary theorists on sheets of foolscap."[9]

Military might and aspirations aside, the *Chicago Tribune* still determined Canada's dismal future lay in the folly of agreeing to a constitutional monarchy instead of embracing republicanism. While royalty might bring with it style, titled counts and dukes were exactly who immigrants were fleeing from — and in the end, it would be the United States, not Canada, that would benefit from keeping the monarchy. "The two systems [republic and constitutional monarchy] are so entirely different," wrote the *Tribune*, "and the one so vastly superior in all things... that

Canada can never hope to be anything more than she now is — a helpless, hopeless, aimless dependent, without a present and without a future, other than a blank in history, and a blank in all things."[10] Except that is, when it came to general news. For a country deemed to be "blank," the *Chicago Tribune* and *New York Times* found a lot to report on.

Shooting Affray Between Brothers in Canada.

PERTH, C. W., Friday, March 1.

In a dispute about the keys of their store last evening, between Capt. J. McG. CHAMBERS and his brother, Dr. CHAMBERS, father of the Member of Parliament for Brockville, the Captain called his brother a liar, whereupon the latter drew a revolver and shot the Captain through the breast, inflicting a dangerous and probably a fatal wound. The Doctor has been arrested.

A typical news dispatch sent from Canada in the 1860s and early '70s. Topics ranged from crop yields and transatlantic ship arrivals to crime stories. (*New York Times*, 2 March 1867)

GENERAL NEWS

At the time of Dominion, regular and often daily dispatches were sent to both the *Chicago Tribune* and the *New York Times* from unnamed sources in Toronto, Montreal, and Ottawa. The notes were compiled in short columns with none-too-inventive titles — the "From Canada" column appeared in the *Tribune* while the *Times* printed its "Canada" column. Tidbits of information covered a wide variety of topics from the collapse of railway bridges to floods, shootings, ships arriving from Liverpool, even a murder case where a mother killed her five children with an axe.

With its city's focus on agriculture and commodities, the *Chicago Tribune* printed articles about crop yields, exports, cattle dying of hunger, and the "invasion" of the Canada thistle. "Canada has always had the advantage of us in matters of reciprocity," wrote an exasperated *Tribune* reporter on 20 November 1871. "Our Fenians went over the line into Her Majesty's dominions and came back again. Their thistles came over the line into our dominions and have stayed and multiplied...."[11] Calling the thistle "everything but fire-proof," the paper reported on efforts in Illinois to get rid of it including a law passed in the state legislature authorizing counties and towns to destroy the spiky, resilient weed.[12]

When it came to newsworthiness in New York, stories of murders and shootings in Canada peppered the *Times*. Fires were also dutifully covered. In the summer of 1868, wildfires ripped through Ontario from north of Lake Superior to the shores of Georgian Bay. The *Times* printed four sentences on a "fire in the woods in Canada" near the town of Stayner, 38 kilometres (24 miles) west of Barrie.[13] The paper reported the blaze destroyed eleven houses, a railway station, and a culvert. One would be hard-pressed to find this kind of detailed coverage for such a seemingly small event in today's mainstream American press, where it appears more lines of print are given to Canadian actors than actions.

As if Canada weren't already fighting the stereotype of being a cold, inhospitable clime, both the *Chicago Tribune* and *New York Times* further propagated the "Canada is the coldest place on earth" theme with headlines such as these: "The Cold Weather in Canada" and the "Intense Cold in Canada," the latter story being only one sentence long and suggesting by its very brevity the harshness of the winter — or perhaps that the telegraph line had frozen.

Despite the lack of details, it remains that in the first few years surrounding Canadian Confederation, reports were printed almost every day of happenings there. But the columns dedicated to the minutiae of Canadian events largely disappeared by 1871. It's unclear whether this decision was made because of a lack of correspondents sending dispatches or disinterest from readers. Either way, it foreshadowed a decline over the next century in Canadian coverage — except when the story was too large to ignore.

BEWARE THE FENIANS

> We are the Fenian Brotherhood, skilled in the arts of war,
> And we're going to fight for Ireland, the land we adore,
> Many battles we have won, along with the boys in blue,
> And we'll go and capture Canada, for we've nothing else to do.
>
> ~ *Fenian soldier's song*

The first direct military challenge to Canada's sovereignty came in the form of Irish-proud Civil War veterans. Between 1866 and 1871, the Fenian Brotherhood staged raids on Canada from New Brunswick to Manitoba. Their plan was to take Canada hostage and use the captured territory as a negotiation tool in securing Ireland's independence from Britain. In the end, the failed attempts made Canada stronger by pushing the provinces to accept Confederation and proving that Canada's part-time volunteer militia could defend itself.

At the end of May 1866, the Fenians launched what would become their largest raid, one that saw them cross the border at Buffalo, New York, and defeat a nine-hundred-strong band of Canadians at Ridgeway near Fort Erie. In the months before the attack, the *New York Times* kept busy chronicling preparations on both sides of the border. Dispatches from Ottawa told of two thousand militia volunteers descending on the city and being billeted to households.[14] As the attack got underway, the *Times* and the *Chicago Tribune* breathlessly reported the skirmishes. "Decisive Battle Expected at Erie To-Day," blared a headline in the *Tribune* on 3 June. The *Times* was one step ahead that day, devoting headline space to this: "Fenians Said to be Throwing Away Arms and Taking to Legs."

Unfortunately for readers, the newspaper reports were already old. By 3 June, the Fenians were hightailing it back to the United States. Another group would cross the border into Quebec a few days later, but quickly retreat and surrender to American forces, which had been instructed to arrest Fenians for breaking U.S. neutrality laws. For the Fenians who had escaped injury, death, or imprisonment, the *Chicago Tribune* wrote it was time they "betake themselves to some honest calling, and reflect that they have postponed the day of Ireland's independence a long time by their blundering and wicked raid upon a people who are in no way responsible for the wrongs of Ireland."[15] For once the paper seemed supportive of Canada, if only to prove a point to its own citizens that rogue elements in the United States would not be tolerated.

But that wasn't the end of the Fenians. In May 1870, General John O'Neill led another raid on Canada. This time the newspapers were quick to proclaim the endeavour a disaster. Reporting that more than a thousand men had gathered in St. Albans, Vermont, as well as Buffalo and Malone, New York, the *Tribune* scoffed at O'Neill's efforts, saying that he had enlisted "fools in an enterprise of brigandage and land piracy"[16] who against blatant disregard of American law were "blindly, and on mere bedlamite impulse, pursuing a folly as bloody as it is stupid."[17] When O'Neill's attempt failed, as the paper had predicted, *Tribune* editors headlined the raid "The Fizzle in Vermont."[18] Except for a brief skirmish in 1871 at Pembina, North Dakota, near the Manitoba border, the Fenian movement had collapsed and Canada — with the help of American authorities — had repelled the invaders.

THE FENIAN WAR.

A Small Skirmish at Ridgeway, Near Fort Erie.

Conflicting Stories of the Affair and the Result.

Both Sides Victorious and Both Sides Whipped.

The Fenians Begin with Success and End with Fight.

British Regulars Marching Rapidly to the Scene.

Reports from the front lines of the Fenian raids on Canada were carried by the *New York Times* and the *Chicago Tribune.* (*New York Times,* 3 June 1866)

From the *New York Times'* perspective, by 1870 the raids were an annoyance. "When we consider the embarrassing position in which these recurring demonstrations put our own authorities," wrote the paper, "and the possible injuries which may be inflicted upon the innocent Canadian people, we certainly fail to appreciate the wisdom or the justification of the movements now being made."[19] Despite the press leading up to the initial raids, it became clear the Fenians had conducted themselves in an amateur fashion that resulted in more rumours and general uproar than actual fighting on either side of the border.

The only positive outcome of these failed Celtic forays, at least in the *Times*' opinion, was the creation of the Dominion of Canada and Britain recalling its troops. Canada's weakness, the paper argued, had stemmed from it being under the protection of the Union Jack. "Henceforth Canada must be answerable for its own defence, at least in time of peace," said the *Times*.[20] The Fenian raids had brought Canadians together, but with a scattered population of mere millions could they defend themselves against threats of annexation?   .

STOKING FEARS OF ANNEXATION

If there has been one enduring and overriding fear among Canadians, it is that of annexation. Shrugged off today as an irrational fear based on dusty war plots and outdated notions of "manifest destiny," in the infant days of Dominion the threat seemed real, especially if one read American newspapers. There in a world bound by ink and margins, a fierce debate took place over how best to gain control of the provinces.

Despite perpetuated stereotypes of Canada's harsh climate and backwardness, some Americans desired the country for its seemingly infinite resources. "The gold, coal, and fisheries o[f] Nova Scotia, the great timber regions and water privileges of New Brunswick, and the vast agricultural resources of Canada would tend largely to augment our national wealth," wrote the *Chicago Tribune* in December 1867, just five months after Canadians celebrated their first Dominion Day.[21] But the person writing the *Tribune* article wasn't only thinking of the benefits to the United States. The journalist had the interests of its conquered souls in mind too. The Canadians, the article stated, would "add strength and stability to our government and institutions, and at the same time push themselves half a century ahead in all their industrial and commercial interests."[22] From the American viewpoint, annexation was a win-win situation. And at the time, the idea appeared quite realistic.

It did not escape notice by the Americans that British Columbia and Nova Scotia were balking against Confederation. In 1867, the *Chicago Tribune* reported on "best authority" that citizens in both areas were clamouring for annexation to the United States. Less than a year later, Nova Scotia threatened to secede from the Dominion. The Canadian government pacified the province with funds from the national treasury and subsidies to build a rail line connecting it to Ontario and Quebec. British Columbia was also mollified with promises of a transcontinental railway when it joined Confederation in 1871.

While Canadians debated the merits of Confederation, the *New York Times* printed a letter penned by *Chicago Tribune* managing editor Joseph Medill to General John Rawlins, a confidant of newly elected President Ulysses Grant. It was early January 1869 and Rawlins was a few months shy of becoming Secretary of War in the president's administration. In his letter, Medill endorsed remarks uttered by Rawlins that hinted at manifest destiny and the annexation of the Canadian provinces. "By the doctrine of 'nationalities' and natural frontiers, that country should be ours, and some day will be," wrote Medill, who ironically was born in Saint John, New Brunswick.[23] Annexation logically made sense he argued, as the Canadians shared the same language, religion, and currency. In practical matters of trade, annexation would abolish the need for customs and in the process, end smuggling operations. Medill proposed that Grant offer Britain one hundred million dollars for the colonies when he became president and if England rejected that proposition, then force would be required and the money offered in a peace treaty. "Sound the bugle, and enough of the old veterans will rally in a month to sweep the Dominion as fast as they can march over it," he wrote.[24]

The controversial statements stirred up the Canadian and American press; so much so that Medill was forced to defend his views in a letter to the *New York Times*, and argue that the note to Rawlins was written as one to a personal friend and never intended for publication.[25] The *Times* — now positioned in the role of referee — published a response from the *Toronto Globe*. Outraged by the dismissive disregard of Canadians' thoughts on the matter of annexation, the *Globe*'s editorial sought a tough stance. "We are quite aware of the lust for empire and territory characteristic of republics, of which Mr. MEDILL speaks so complacently, " it said, "and can only say that even if a very strong man tries to break into a house, its owner has no alternative but to give him as warm a reception as possible."[26] The *Globe* never had to make good on its threat, as President Grant didn't take up Medill's proposal. Along with Secretary of State Hamilton Fish, the president preferred a "wait and see" approach, convinced the Confederation couldn't survive on its own and annexation would naturally occur.

Still, political circles were abuzz with talk of annexing Canada. In 1869, Senator Zachariah Chandler from Michigan vocally advocated that the United States tell Britain it would accept Canada as settlement in the *Alabama* claims. This unresolved dispute stemmed from the Civil War when Confederate warships, disguised as merchant vessels, were built in Britain and used by the South to capture and sink Union ships. The American government argued Britain had violated neutrality laws by building the boats and demanded compensation for the losses it had suffered. Interestingly, the *Chicago Tribune* opposed the idea of using Canada as a pawn to settle the *Alabama* claims. Arguing that annexation sentiment was rising in Canada, the paper advocated another position — leave Canada alone, "cease shaking your fists at them, and they will seek annexation of their own accord. In other words, we shall get them for nothing."[27] While Medill had earlier urged for brute annexation, the *Tribune* regarded Chandler's idea as "undemocratic" and a "denial of popular rights."[28] In defence of Canada, the paper wrote that Canadians "are entitled like ourselves and like the people of England to exercise self-government. They are not mere chattels, to be sold like quadroon slaves to pay the debts of their parent."[29] Canada, it seemed, was not to be used as a bargaining chip unless the proposal met Medill's approval.

The *Chicago Tribune* continued pushing its agenda through 1870, writing in one article that Canada would benefit from having a delegation of senators and representatives in Congress instead of being left in the "wet and cold."[30] In another story, the paper reported that Canada's willingness to "hang on the imperial skirts" was fatal to the country's future prosperity.[31] The only solution, said the *Tribune*, was for Britain to voluntarily cut all ties with her provinces or for Canada to assert her independence. "The road out of the great slough of despond in which the Canadas have so long floundered is Independence," wrote the paper. "So long as they remain British provinces they will remain what they are — nobody."[32] Visually underscoring that pervasive viewpoint were the scores of Canadians crossing the border.

CANADIAN EXODUS

If annexation remained an elusive reality, the Americans pressing for it could feel some vindication in the sheer number of immigrants bidding adieu to the British dominion and saying howdy to their republic. In 1868, the *Chicago Tribune* estimated that 90 percent of the immigrants landing in the provinces eventually moved to America.[33] A year later, it stated that fewer than 5 percent of European immigrants stayed in Canada for more than six months.[34] These numbers seem highly exaggerated when compared to conventional wisdom that places this figure at roughly one-third of immigrants ultimately ending up in the United States.[35]

Either way, it can't be denied that the U.S. received a great many emigrants from Canada. In words echoed throughout the following centuries, the *Tribune* attributed the mass migration to those Canadians who "having any ambition to better their condition, move off to the States, and leave the Provinces to vegetate and decay, in sight of the universal prosperity and increase in every State on the opposite side of the lakes."[36] As soon as people were of legal age, asserted the *Tribune*, they set course to the land of the free. They "shake the dust of the decayed and decaying provinces from their feet," wrote the paper, "and cast their lot with the homogeneous race which, in the States of American Union, are enjoying freedom, liberty, prosperity and have a future before them for themselves and for their children."[37] It's doubtful American ideals of freedom and liberty were critical factors in the decision-making process for a majority of emigrants as many were loyal to Britain. But jobs and wages — that was another story. From the 1840s until 1930, approximately two million English-speaking Canadians headed south, lured by the promise of golden economic opportunities.[38] During that same time, roughly one million French Canadians headed to industrial cities in the Northeast seeking factory work.

A lack of arable land also pushed Canadians across the border. In 1872, a correspondent for the *New York Times* travelled to the Parry Sound and Muskoka areas of Ontario where the Canadian government was handing out free land grants of one hundred to two hundred acres. It was noted that many recently arrived immigrants were rejecting the offer and continuing on to the Western states through Detroit. After visiting "the backwoods of Canada," the reporter knew why. Sure it was free —"But such land!" exclaimed the correspondent. "Acres of rock and rods of soil, and the better the soil the denser the forest."[39] With backbreaking labour needed to clear the land and pithy yields the reward, the free-grant districts held no appeal for farmers who could get far greater returns in the American West.

As Canadians packed up and headed out, the *New York Times* quoted anonymous writers and newspaper editors in Halifax, Montreal, and New Brunswick detailing the exodus. "Twenty-five families from my neighborhood will leave this Spring for the United States, and each family will take with them from $800 to $1,400, in gold," wrote a Canadian in New Brunswick. "As many more would leave if they could sell their farms, and procure money to carry them away."[40] In Montreal, the *Witness* described what was happening in the parishes south of the St. Lawrence. "Many families are emigrating without even caring to dispose of their farms," said the paper. "They nail boards across windows and doors, and start, without any other means but those furnished them by their friends who have gone before."[41]

Whether it was to the field or factory, thousands of Canadians crossed the border during the first years of Dominion and started new lives in the United States. As with other immigrants arriving in the pursuit of prosperity, Americans welcomed them. The *Chicago Tribune* did so grudgingly. "These people are somewhat primitive in many things," it sniffed, "but they are honest, virtuous and industrious, and, with these qualities, will not fail in this country."[42]

With those same values, the Canadians who stayed in the Dominion didn't fail their own country either. Heading into and entering the twentieth century, Canada urbanized, industrialized, and expanded, adding the provinces of Prince Edward Island, Alberta, and Saskatchewan, as well as the Yukon Territory. With the signing of the Treaty of Washington in 1871, disputes over the *Alabama* claims, boundary, fishing rights, and navigation of the St. Lawrence were resolved. With little to argue over, public swipes at Canada died down in the American press. Then along came the reciprocity treaty in 1911.

★★★ **CHAPTER 2** ★★★

FREE TRADE OR "FREEDOM"

1911

> To say that the interests of Canada and the United States
> are opposed is as absurd as to say that one man cannot sleep
> because some one else, somewhere else is sleeping and so
> using up all the sleep. ~ *J. Laurence Laughlin*[1]

By 1911, Canada's growing prosperity and increasing trade
with the United States brought both governments to the
negotiating table in Washington, D.C. The goal was to hammer
out a reciprocity treaty, or free trade agreement as it would be
called today. The two countries had first signed such a treaty
in 1854. But by 1866, the United States had terminated the
agreement in an effort to help American farmers after the Civil
War.[2] Prominent Canadians including the country's first prime
minister, Sir John A. Macdonald, actively sought a new treaty
throughout the following decades and made pilgrimages to
Washington without any luck. Until now.

On 7 January 1911, Finance Minister William Fielding and
Customs Minister William Paterson arrived in Washington.
These two men, wrote the *New York Times*, would be doing
the "real work of negotiating for Canada."[3] The Canadian
delegation included four more members of Prime Minister Sir
Wilfrid Laurier's Liberal cabinet. Unlike past administrations,
President William Taft was keen to strike a deal.

Trade was brisk between the Republic and the Dominion. The *New York Times* reported that by 1910, 37.54 percent of Canada's exports were shipped to the United States while 59.47 percent of Canada's imports came from it.[4] Total trade between the two countries was now more than three hundred fifty million dollars, with two hundred thirty-three million dollars of that being American exports to the Dominion.[5] From a purely economic perspective, lowering and eliminating duties on products seemed advantageous to parties on both sides of the border. Generally, the United States desired Canada's raw materials such as its lumber, wood pulp, and grains while Canada wanted cheaper access to manufactured goods, including farm supplies.

The mere news that reciprocity and closer ties to Canada were being discussed led at least one major American newspaper to raise the red flag of annexation. Although admitting the idea had lost popular appeal, a *Boston Globe* article reprinted in the *Washington Post* outlined the potentially destructive choices Canada faced with free trade. If Canadians' demands for reciprocity were not met, it said, "there is danger that demand for annexation with the United States will be made persistently, and if reciprocity is granted then the close relations between the two countries may bring about a desire for national unity. Either horn of the dilemma points to an eventual merger."[6]

While some Americans spoke matter-of-factly of inevitable union, across the border Clifford Sifton, a Liberal MP and former minister of the interior in Laurier's cabinet, was resolutely railing against reciprocity. In a hint of what was to come, Sifton addressed a Canadian Club luncheon saying that now "is not the time to take down the bars of trade and turn Canada's natural resources over to the United States. The best way of continuing good relations between Canada and the United States is that each should do its own business independently and have no entanglements, nothing in the world to quarrel about."[7] The crowd of senators, members of Parliament, prominent businessmen, and bankers cheered loudly, reported the journalist covering the event for the *Washington Post*. Clearly, Sifton's views didn't reflect those held by his leader.

Two weeks into the free trade negotiations, the American and Canadian delegates reached an agreement. Reciprocal free lists were published in the *Washington Post* and *Wall Street Journal* on 27 January listing products that would now be "free"— wheat, fruit, eggs, cottonseed oil, and terne plates — and those products whose duties were to be reduced — bacon, lard, satchels, clocks, plows, and drills.

The *Chicago Tribune* breathed a sigh of relief. The existence of duties, it wrote, "is an absurdity where conditions as to production and wages on one side of the boundary are essentially the same as those on the other side."[8] In an about-turn from its calls for annexation just forty years earlier, the paper glowingly described Canada as a "great and growing country."

But the reciprocity agreement was one of agreed principle, not automatic enactment. The measure had to be submitted simultaneously to Parliament and Congress for approval, and as any deals regarding reciprocity affected the tariff law, both the United States House of Representatives and the Senate had to ratify it. That would prove to be a problem with just five weeks remaining until the end of the current session of Congress. Farmers, lumberjacks, and fishermen loudly expressed disapproval, citing lower prices under the new arrangement. The *Washington Post*, with its base in the Capitol, mocked the farmers' concerns. Urging them to consider interests other than commodity futures and livestock prices, the paper argued that good relations between Canada and the United States "would be fostered by giving Canada a whack at the markets of the American farmer. Canada would feel better, less belligerent, less likely to attack the United States."[9] Though admitting the two countries were on friendly terms, the *Post* cautioned, "no one knows when the dogs of war may show their teeth."[10]

Now it seemed there were more threats coming from within Congress than elsewhere. Despite President Taft sending a special message and arguing that free trade would lower the cost of living for all Americans, the reciprocity bill was stalled. On 8 February, the president issued an ultimatum — if the agreement died in this congressional session, he would call a special one to ratify it. "As the Democrats say they would ignore reciprocity were an extra session called, and as the Republicans insist that reciprocity is seen to be too radical a departure from the protection principle to be acted on hastily," wrote the *Washington Post*, "the grim specter is in evidence whichever way the Canadian baby turns."[11] With no clear voice coming from Congress, the newspapers quickly filled the gap.

RNING, FEBRUARY 10, 1911.—TWELVE PAGES.

THE STATUE OF PEACE THAT CAME TO LIFE.

An editorial cartoon published in the *Des Moines Register* depicts the political stalemate in Congress over the 1911 reciprocity agreement – and President William Taft's not-so-subtle push for its ratification. (*Des Moines Register*, 10 February 1911)

If the president's reciprocity measure were defeated, the *Chicago Tribune* boldly stated, it would be because Americans and Congress were "pusillanimous and purblind."[12] The paper unequivocally supported passage of reciprocity, arguing this issue involved "not only the largest material good of two great peoples but likewise the largest social and moral good. We know, or we ought to know, in this twentieth century that civilization and social advancement move on the great current of commerce."[13] If opponents to reciprocity were standing behind protectionism, the paper seemed determined to defend its views with an equally high-minded ideal.

In New York, the *Wall Street Journal* printed an opinion piece written by James J. Hill, a prominent American free trade backer and president of the Northern Pacific Railroad. Hill, who was born in Eramosa Township, Ontario, linked reciprocity to civilization by invoking the legendary images of the missionary and voyageur. Saying that the wilderness was gone and "savage life is no more," he declared it was time for Canada and the United States to break down barriers. International understanding and reciprocity "are the forerunners of a more enlightened age," Hill wrote. "By their efforts a new and better regime is to be established among the nations. It is the part of these pioneer governments to blaze the trail."[14] But somewhere in the tangled woods of Congress, politicians put down the axe and stopped clearing a path for Hill's trail, if they'd even been bushwhacking one in the first place. While the House of Representatives passed the reciprocity measure, the Senate adjourned without bringing it to a vote.

"CHAMP CLARK'S BOMBSHELL"

Of all the comments and hyperbole presented in Congress during the rush to pass the reciprocity measure, Representative James Beauchamp "Champ" Clark of Missouri gave what would arguably become a most damaging, yet for some papers, highly amusing statement about Canada. During bitter debate on the House floor before the bill was passed, Clark declared, "I look forward to the time when the American flag will fly over every square foot of British North America, up to the north pole.

The people of Canada are of our blood and our language."[15] The press had a field day with this comment. Could it be possible, mused the *Washington Post*, that the anti-Canadian remarks actually helped push the measure through the House? The Congressional Record noted "prolonged applause" from Democrats when Clark finished speaking.[16] "Evidently, then," wrote the *Post*, "the Democrats generally approved of Mr. Clark's annexation sentiments, and voted for the reciprocity bill because, among other things, it improves the prospect of annexation."[17] With the Democrats wielding a House majority in the upcoming 62nd Congress and Clark elected as its Speaker, the paper said it wouldn't blame Canadians if they regarded the bill's passage as a first step toward annexation.

In Chicago, the *Tribune* rebuked Clark, saying the soon-to-be Speaker's comments were unacceptable even if they were meant as a joke. The paper was worried about how Canadians might interpret the representative's exuberant *faux pas*. "He let his imagination run wild like a Missouri mule on the rampage," it wrote. "Remarks about the absorption of one country by another grate harshly on the ears of the people of the smaller."[18]

Further embarrassing the Taft administration, two days after Clark's remarks, Republican Representative William Bennet of New York introduced resolutions in the House calling for the president to start negotiations with Britain to annex Canada. Taft spoke immediately with the chairman of the foreign relations committee and asked him to take a vote. The resolutions failed nine to one with Bennet the only member in favour of them.[19] Interestingly, he had voted against the reciprocity bill a few days earlier, leading some reciprocity advocates and later some historians to believe that Bennet, along with other protectionists, purposely spoke of annexation to stir up Canadian opposition to the agreement.[20]

The calls for annexation on the House floor, whether serious or superficial, rallied Canada's Conservative opposition party led by Sir Robert Borden. Clark's and Bennet's actions, reported the *Washington Post*, had "roused the opponents of reciprocity in and out of parliament to the highest pitch of excitement they have yet reached."[21] The Conservatives argued that the Liberals under Laurier's leadership were taking the first tentative step in breaking the ties that bound the Dominion to the British Empire.

The *Post* article also reported that outside Parliament, a swell of anti-Americanism was being reflected in the media as well as in the arts. "Anti-American sentiment is showing itself in many amusing ways," stated the dispatch from Ottawa. "An American theatrical company using some American flags in 'The Jolly Bachelors' at the Princess Theater, in Montreal last night, got the tip from an anti-reciprocity newspaper to remove the colors. One leading Canadian paper tonight prints pictures of the parliament buildings here with American flags flying from them."[22]

The *Los Angeles Times* picked up the story too, quoting anti-American sentiment in the *Montreal Daily Star*, one of the most widely circulated Canadian papers at the time. The *Star* appealed to Laurier to rethink his stance on reciprocity, arguing that any agreement would deal a severe blow to the development of Canada by isolating its provinces and stifling emerging industries. The only true winner in this deal, it said, would be the Taft administration, which had so actively pursued it. "None of us realized the inward meaning of the shrewdly framer offer of the long head American government when we first saw it," positioned the *Star*. "It was as cunning a trap as was ever laid. The master bargainers at Washington have not lost their skill."[23]

But the idea that the Americans were surreptitiously swindling Canadians into annexation or a bad deal through reciprocity perplexed the *Times*. The paper likened free trade to a game of swap. Sure one country could get stuck with the worst part of a bargain, but it could also receive the best of it. And the Dominion, the *Times* argued, was likely to receive the latter. A Canadian, it reminded its readers, "is not a stage Britisher with a slipped-down chest and a checker-board vest, who is shy of his h's and who is cheated by a beaver-hatted, chin-goateed, nasal-voiced stage Yankee. The Canuck has grafted upon his British stock the alertness and snap of his American neighbor, and if he gets the worst of it in any trade with Uncle Sam it will astonish those who know him."[24]

Over at the *Washington Post*, the outcry against reciprocity from newspapers and Conservatives in Canada was dealt with more pragmatically. The Canadian Parliament was different from Congress, it stated and even if Champ Clark were to ride up to Ottawa "with his mules, Reciprocity and Annexation," not a vote would change among the Liberal Party, which held a majority by twenty-five seats in Parliament. Canadian politicians were "as responsive to the crack of the party whip as a British jury is to the will of the judge," wrote the paper. "There is no diversity of opinion, such as we have witnessed in Congress, where each angle of the proposition drew to it a following of its own, like so many rallying points on the floor of the stock exchange."[25] With its mind settled that the reciprocity agreement was assured passage in the House of Commons, the *Post* turned its attention back to Congress, where members in support of and against reciprocity were readying themselves for another tense battle to secure votes — this time in a special session called by President Taft.

ROUND TWO FOR RECIPROCITY

When Congress convened for the extra session on 4 April, President Taft sent another special message. Citing public approval and a promise by the two countries' representatives to use their "utmost efforts to bring about the tariff changes," he urged ratification of the reciprocity agreement.[26] Two and a half weeks later Democrats pushed the measure through the House of Representatives. Now it was back to the Senate. Once again, the bill became entangled in bitter debates over protectionism and the potential threat of free trade to the agricultural, fishing, lumber, and print paper industries. There was also concern about whether the "favoured nation" clause in commercial treaties with Germany, Britain, and France restricted the United States' ability to enact a reciprocity agreement with Canada. In mid-April, such concern was deemed unfounded based on a Customs Court decision involving British whisky.

In the months leading up to the Senate vote, many major newspapers sided with Taft in urging quick ratification of the reciprocity measure. At the *New York Times*, it was argued that duties had placed the Canadian market at an artificial distance. "The tariff charge is more burdensome than the railway rate schedule, and a greater hindrance than the elevations of the mountain ranges which must be crossed in going between the oceans," the paper wrote. "The leveling of the barriers between the northward and southward movement of traffic costs nothing but the price of paper and ink and the trouble of overcoming ancient preconceptions."[27]

In Chicago, the *Tribune* echoed President Taft's view that the free trade agreement had to be considered in "now or never" terms. Choosing "now" would be the "statesmanlike seizure of a golden opportunity which, if slighted, never would return," it said. "The rejection of reciprocity would be a finality. Canada would be thrown irrevocably into the arms of Great Britain, commercially speaking."[28] The *Tribune* pressed upon Americans to at the very least give free trade a chance, a trial period to see if it worked.

The *Washington Post* agreed. With Taft's statements being examined and torn apart on the Senate floor, prolonged conversations "as to consistency and inconsistency can serve no good end," the paper stated. "A vote that will end the discussion is what the country wants."[29] Out in California, the *Los Angeles Times* also advocated for a close to the discussions, but it had a different objective in mind. It wanted the bill to die.

"NO" FROM THE GOLDEN COAST

With its border hugging Mexico, not Canada, the *Los Angeles Times* saw in reciprocity a threat to Californians' livelihood. They feared that if free trade were established with America's neighbour to the north, a similar agreement could not be denied to its "sister republic" to the south — and that could destroy the citrus industry in the Golden State. In statements strongly resembling concerns uttered in California nearly a century later when Mexican avocados entered the United States under the North American Free Trade Agreement, the *Times* argued that with reciprocity, "the product of the Mexican orchards, cultivated by peon labor, would drive California fruit out of the eastern markets, and our orchardists could cut down their trees and cultivate alfalfa and sugar beets instead."[30]

It wasn't just that the *Times* was wary of cross-border competition; it didn't see any benefit for California in a free trade agreement with Canada. The Eastern regions that had been stripped of their expansive forests might desire cheap lumber, but the redwoods in Alaska and Washington, and the pines in California's Sierras could supply all the timber needs for the West Coast. When it came to the supply of food essentials, the Golden State was too far away to benefit from cheaper products. And so, engaging humorous imagery and unbridled enthusiasm, the Los Angeles Times fought the reciprocity agreement with every drop of its ink-based editorial being.

Using Bureau of Statistics reports, the Times examined exports and imports during the twelve years of the 1854 reciprocity treaty and found that while exports to Canada remained roughly the same, imports from Canada had increased substantially. Writer Walter Ballard took these notes:

> The game was not worth the candle, particularly as it left us in 1866 where we were in 1854, twelve years before, with exports of only $24,000,000, while in the period our imports from Canada rose from $9,000,000 to $48,000,000, or more than five times as much. Which country gained by that twelve years of reciprocity, Canada or the United States? The answer is obvious and greatly to our loss.[31]

Ballard also analysed trade figures in the six years prior to 1911, which recorded that American exports to Canada increased by more than 50 percent despite tariffs. "With this showing of actual facts (not theories)," he wrote, "there is not a microscope in existence powerful enough to discern any trade advantage to us in the present proposed treaty, or agreement as it is called, of reciprocity with Canada...."[32]

The paper itself argued that the Dominion's extensive undeveloped agricultural resources posed a threat to American farmers and that the United States would be giving Canada access to millions more customers while it gained a much smaller market share in return. Americans were being asked "to make Canada a present of a market advantage of nearly twelve to one," asserted the Times. "What business man, on either side of the line, would make, without consideration, a contract in his business which would give the other party such an enormous advantage as that? The idea is preposterous."[33]

Along with its rational number-heavy defence against free trade, the *Times* readily poked fun at Canadians, who were already flooding into the state by the thousands as "snowbirds" during the winter months. Quoting an article in the *Victoria Times* that spoke of a day when the northern "Colossus, sleeping as yet, will throw a shadow over the North American continent," the *Los Angeles Times* chided the Canadian paper for its immodest behaviour.[34] Then it wrote this cheeky reply:

> We await with unfeigned sorrow the inevitable hour when the American eagle will "seek shelter" under the wings of the Canadian bantam; when the lion of the South shall silence his roar and listen respectfully to the chipper of the northern chipmunk; when Kentucky horses shall be distanced on the race track of nations by Canadian Shetland ponies. If our inevitable fate is to be annexed to the Colossus of the North let us delay the calamity as long as possible and not hasten it by reciprocity.[35]

It was obvious journalists at the *Times* revelled in the use of humour when delivering a political punch line. "The people of 'Our Lady of the Snows' or 'The Colossus of the North,' as the Canadian Dominion is poetically and variously designated, are anxiously awaiting the fate of the reciprocity treaty," said another *Times* article. "But, but, but our selfish motto as to Canada is that of Louis the Eleventh: 'Honor the church, but give it nothing.'"[36]

On 22 July, senators on Capitol Hill did the opposite. After five months of harsh debate in Congress, the Senate passed the reciprocity bill without amendment by a vote of 53 to 27. The *Washington Post* called it the bitterest fight for legislation by an administration in years. The *Wall Street Journal* labelled it a triumph for President Taft and the *New York Times* praised the president's wisdom and courage. In a political move that would be unacceptable today but highlighted the undeniable influence of the American press, Taft sent a message to the Hearst newspaper conglomerate congratulating them for their role in helping to ensure the reciprocity agreement's passage through Congress.[37]

THE "COLOSSUS."

"Canada," says the Victoria (B. C.) Times, "is rightly denominated the Colossus of the North. Her potential greatness can be made to make the greatness of America look pygmean when compared. Some day this Colossus, sleeping as yet, will throw a shadow over the North American continent under which the other part of the continent may be glad to seek snelter."

"Modesty," says the proverb, "is a quality which highly adorns a woman but is utterly ruinous to a man." It is obvious that ruin will never be precipitated upon "Our Lady of the Snows" in consequence of the shrinking diffidence of her newspaper press. The Times has hitherto been of the opinion that there were newspapers in Southern California capable of expressing high appreciation of our climate, our resources and our growth. But we must all take off our hats to this British Columbia booster. He is the limit. He is IT.

We await with unfeigned sorrow the inevitable hour when the American eagle will "seek shelter" under the wings of the Canadian bantam; when the lion of the South shall silence his roar and listen respectfully to the chipper of the northern chipmunk, when Kentucky horses shall be distanced on the race track of nations by Canadian Shetland ponies. If our inevitable fate is to be annexed to the Colossus of the North let us delay the calamity as long as possible and not hasten it by reciprocity.

The *Los Angeles Times* revels in vivid imagery in this sassy response to the idea of Canada as the "Colossus of the North." (*Los Angeles Times*, 12 June 1911)

The president and his administration had come through on their promise. Now it was up to Prime Minister Sir Wilfrid Laurier and his Liberal Party in Canada to deliver theirs.

THE FIGHT FOR FREE TRADE IN CANADA

With the reciprocity issue resolved in the United States, the American press turned its full attention north. There, reciprocity had muddled Parliament much the same way it had Congress. Prime Minister Sir Wilfrid Laurier was "having the fight of his career to carry reciprocity at all," wrote the *New York Times*.[38] To keep the free trade bill from coming to a vote, opposition members under the leadership of Sir Robert Borden had deployed a tactic unavailable to their counterparts in the House of Representatives — a filibuster. That left Laurier with two options: withdraw the reciprocity measure, or dissolve Parliament and call a general election. The prime minister chose the latter and an election was set for 21 September. The American press took note. "Exciting Times in Canada," ran a headline in the *Washington Post*. It's likely that never before had the United States "been so vitally interested, materially and otherwise, in the result of an election in a foreign country as attaches to the pending struggle," wrote the *Post*. "Hitherto but scant interest has been displayed in the ups and downs of political control in Canada."[39] American interest was high because if the Liberals were returned to power with a majority of seats in the House of Commons, the reciprocity agreement was almost certain to be approved. If however, the Conservatives won the election, any hopes of free trade would be dashed. The "now or never" argument used in the United States applied to Canada as well.

The Conservatives had been voicing opposition to the reciprocity agreement for months already, with one member even going so far as to compare Finance Minister William Fielding and President Taft to Samson and Delilah, with Fielding having "succumbed to Presidential blandishments."[40] The statement was criticized by papers in Western Canada and caused uproar among settlers there who had come from the United States. Now with an election date set, the *Washington Post* expected a bitter fight for the votes of Canadians. The opponents of reciprocity had "already set up the campaign cry of 'American gold and annexation,'" wrote the *Post*, "and doubtless the Champ Clark bugaboo will be dangled from every stump in the Dominion."[41]

The paper's predictions proved accurate as Borden focused his campaign attacks on reciprocity. Arguing that free trade would "Americanize" Canada and sever the nation's loyal ties to the British Empire, Conservatives rallied Canadians to stand up for their country and its independence. "It is beyond doubt," the *New York Times* quoted Borden as saying during his opening campaign speech in London, Ontario, "that the leading public men of the United States, its leading press, and the mass of its people believe annexation of this Dominion to be the ultimate, inevitable, and desirable result of this proposition, and for that reason support it."[42] Borden's broad statement clearly annoyed the *Chicago Tribune*. The Conservative Party leader may know what Canadians were thinking, but he dare not make assumptions about American thought, the paper huffed. Other than the "occasional exuberant orator with a disorderly imagination," said the *Tribune*, "no American thinks of the absorption of Canada, even as a remote possibility. The commercial results of reciprocity would be great. The political results would be nil."[43]

As the summer weeks of campaigning led into the dappled days of early fall, the American newspapers wrote of increasing anti-Americanism in Canada. A correspondent in Ontario reported that hundreds of thousands of pamphlets containing extracts of the annexation speeches made in Congress were being handed out to newly arrived British immigrants and Canadians loyal to the British Empire.[44] News dispatches from Montreal described the proliferation of anti-American cartoons in newsprint including one of a whisky bottle with the Stars and Stripes as its label and another of Americans rejoicing in Canada's downfall.[45] The anti-annexation cry, wrote the *Los Angeles Times*, "portrays the Americans as a corrupt, bragging, boodle-hunting and negro lynching crowd from which the Canadian workingman and the Canadian land of milk and honey must be saved."[46]

It naturally followed that as a nastier tone appeared in the Canadian papers, so it did in the American ones. A few weeks before the election, Borden told supporters that Canadians had no choice but to reject reciprocity if they wanted to maintain a standard of living that was higher than their neighbours. The *Chicago Tribune* mocked such reasoning. "The Canadians would not ship away to us portions of their standard of national life with their wheat, cabbages, and poultry," said the *Tribune*. "If nations surrender their ideals when they put no restrictions on trade, England must by this time have parted with all her ideals and got in return many strange foreign ones."[47]

Stumping on the campaign trail had become incredibly sentimental as Borden and his Conservatives argued that a vote for reciprocity would mean a vote against Britain. Still, the *Chicago Tribune* held on to the hope that after the flag waving and "claptrap tricks," Canadians would realize that when "all the froth is brushed from Canadian oratory the bottom fact remains and is generally recognized that the dominion needs the United States market for its products."[48] As the paper pointed out, almost 60 percent of Canada's trade was already taking place with the United States despite the tariff restrictions.[49]

Other papers were equally confident that Canadians would cast their ballots for reciprocity and place Laurier's Liberal Party back in power. Days before the election, the *Los Angeles Times* quoted a poll projecting a majority win for the Liberals with thirty-five seats.[50] In the *Washington Post*, a story from Montreal expressed doubt that Borden's Conservatives, with all their America-bashing comments, could upset Laurier's fifteen-year reign as prime minister. "Canada," said the writer, "never has elected a pessimistic party to power."[51] Canadian representatives had repeatedly gone to Washington seeking reciprocity. Now that such an agreement was within their grasp, there was a belief Canadians wouldn't let it flutter to the floor. "It is utterly incredible that Canadians will seize the present occasion to cater to tory hatred of the republic by slapping Uncle Sam in the face," said the writer.[52] But on election day, that's just what voters did.[53]

FALL OF RECIPROCITY

On 21 September, Canadians cast their ballots for Sir Robert Borden and the Conservatives, handing the party a majority of seats in the House of Commons. Sir Wilfrid Laurier and his quest for reciprocity had been rejected. President Taft's great triumph was dead. The president heard of the election results while at a dinner event in Kalamazoo, Michigan. "For me it is a great disappointment," he said, but added, "It takes two to make a bargain, and if Canada declines we can still go on doing business at the old stand."[54] This statement was widely reprinted in newspapers across the country. The unofficial view in Washington, the *New York Times* said, was that there was nothing the administration could do but make the best of the situation.[55] The *Washington Post* echoed that sentiment and those of Taft, writing diplomatically that it was "a pity, of course, that so much effort should have come to naught. But there must be two parties to a bargain, and it is not to the discredit of the United States in any way if Canada sees fit to reject the agreement."[56] Others in the American press weren't so respectful. Whether out of a sense of disappointment, anger, or betrayal, newspaper editorials expressed outrage and disgust:

> Perhaps a consequence as great as any, in its future influence, is the terrible deterioration in Canadian politics. We have seen wealthy and selfish interests here use unscrupulous appeals to popular passion in order to secure ends which would not bear the light of day.... Never was a campaign so lavishly financed, so callously debased; while the only fighting issues, the jingo puerilities of annexation, are too contemptible for serious argument.[58] ~ *Wall Street Journal*

> ... the Canadians have permitted themselves to be fooled and bamboozled against their own interests in regard to the Reciprocity Agreement. Measured by any test of its relation to the prosperity of Canada and its people, the agreement was so advantageous to them that its rejection was regarded as well-nigh incredible. We did not think they would be so foolish.[59] ~ *New York Times*

> Canada has slammed the door in our faces. But as we had been holding the door shut for forty years it hardly behooves us to adopt a very contemptuous attitude. It is true Canada has had the benefit of experience and ought by this time to

know better. Yet there is a certain splendor in her folly. Only a people with the insolent confidence and heedless passion of youth would turn away from such an opportunity — the opportunity freely to trade with 90,000,000 of the richest and most extravagant people on earth.[57] ~ *Chicago Tribune*

Their ballots have consigned to everlasting flames the bogy of annexation to the United States which Champ Clark called from the deeps. It was not really a wraith of anything that ever existed on this side of the line. It was a pumpkin scarehead with blazing eyes, a crooked slit for a nose, and a hideous grinning mouth which the fun-loving Champ placed upon a pole along with the Stars and Stripes, the while he carried terror to the loyal Canuck heart by his derisive shout of annexation.[60] ~ *Los Angeles Times*

CANADA'S VERDICT.

Canada has slammed the door in our faces. But as we had been holding the door shut for forty years it hardly behooves us to adopt a very contemptuous attitude. It is true Canada has had the benefit of experience and ought by this time to know better. Yet there is a certain splendor in her folly. Only a people with the insolent confidence and heedless passion of youth would turn away from such an opportunity—the opportunity freely to trade with 90,000,000 of the richest and most extravagant people on earth.

Of course the talk of annexation was buncombe, unfortunately given color by the untimely jocular chauvinism of Mr. Champ Clark and the possibly calculated echo of Mr. Mann and others in congress. And it is unfortunate that the Conservative campaign in its lack of sound economic reasons should have felt it necessary and found it profitable to work upon national prejudice and inflame national enmity against a friendly neighbor. That is the aspect of the reciprocity episode which is, without mitigation, deplorable.

So far as the failure of the convention is concerned it will please millions of Americans and be of advantage to at least thousands. But as the benefits to be expected by the United States would have been very gradually registered and very broadly spread, disappointment cannot be very keen. The reciprocity measure was one of broad, beneficent, and farseeing statesmanship, certain to work to the advantage of the two peoples, without any of those sinister complications which Conservative chauvinism imagined. But since it is beaten the United States will continue to thrive and Canada will continue to thrive, despite the stupid commercial barrier between us.

Eventually when Canada has learned her lesson that barrier will come down. But this cannot be expected for many years.

President Taft and Premier Laurier attempted a piece of constructive statesmanship. It is nothing to their discredit that it failed. History will honor them for it.

News of a Conservative Party win in Canada and the resulting defeat of the reciprocity agreement prompted editorials expressing dismay, including this one in the *Chicago Tribune*. (*Chicago Tribune*, 23 September 1911)

Debate over why the reciprocity agreement had failed in Canada held the attention of the press for a few weeks. Some of the papers reprinted letters from readers speculating about the *real* reason for the loss. One person, identified by the initials W.S.G., wrote to the *New York Times* that blame should be cast on descendants of the United Empire Loyalists, Americans who were loyal to the British crown and immigrated to Canada during the War of Independence, for they still harboured resentment towards the United States.[61] Tom MacRae had another idea. He wrote to the *Chicago Tribune* that Canadians defeated free trade to satisfy their pride after enduring the humiliation of having repeated appeals for free trade dismissed by Americans in the past.[62] In an effort to settle the matter with its readers, the *Los Angeles Times* reprinted an article from *The Oregonian* listing a number of possible explanations for the reciprocity rejection ending with the kicker, "Because Canada does not like us, anyway."[63]

Regardless the reason, the reciprocity agreement was dead. It would take decades before a comprehensive free trade agreement would emerge with the signing of the Canada–United States Free Trade Agreement in 1988. That in turn led to the North American Free Trade Agreement (NAFTA), an even larger trading bloc including Mexico, in 1994.

JUST BECAUSE.

[The Oregonian·] Some of the reasons why Canada rejected reciprocity will be found to be included in the following:

Because Champ Clark made a foolish speech about annexation.

Because President Taft is not popular in Canada.

Because Canada thought reciprocity would benefit the United States more than Canada.

Because Canada feared that any manifestation of friendliness to the United States would be a demonstration of disloyalty to Great Britain.

Because reciprocity was seen to be widely popular in the United States.

Because the manufacturers of Canada believed their industries were in great peril.

Because Canada could not see how both parties to a trade bargain could profit.

Because of the purpose of a rival leader of the French element to upset Laurier.

Because political thought and action in Canada are provincial, prejudiced and all-sufficient.

Because a political reaction in Canada was about due.

Because Canada does not like us, anyway.

Another article in response to the failure of reciprocity in Canada, as reprinted in the *Los Angeles Times*. (*Los Angeles Times*, 1 October 1911)

CHAPTER 3

CASTRO, NUKES & THE COLD WAR

1953–1968

The relationship of a large and a small power is never long free from irritations. ~ *John M. Lee[1]*

Geography has made us neighbors. History has made us friends. Economics has made us partners; and necessity has made us allies. Those whom nature has so joined together, let no man put asunder. ~ *President John F. Kennedy, Speech to Canadian Parliament, 17 May 1961*

By the early 1950s, Canada and the United States were closer than ever. Increasing cross-border trade and American investment in Canada had fostered further integration, and the economic relationship was now the largest one ever between two countries in the world's history.[2] Militarily, two world wars and the Korean War, which ended in July 1953, had strengthened defence ties.

Well into the 1960s, one issue would push the two countries to co-operate even more — the threat of encroaching communism from both sides of the continent. These were the years of McCarthyism, the Cuban missile crisis during President John F. Kennedy's "Camelot," the Bomarc missile program, and Vietnam. It may seem an era too vast to cover in one chapter. But it's interesting that during this time, major American newspapers printed relatively few articles about the tensions that would arise between Canada and the United States. Even fewer articles could be found that bashed Canada. Perhaps this perceived lack of negativity resulted from journalism's focus on establishing itself as a profession that objectively reported the news. In the past, reporters or editors had anonymously written stories, penning whatever they desired without being held accountable. Now it was the norm for stories to be accompanied by a reporter byline, which in its very nature encouraged greater accuracy and restraint as the journalist's reputation was based on what was written and how those stories were reported.

Although Canadian and American government policy differed widely during this period of the Cold War, newspapers gave these decisions much less attention than they had in 1911 with free trade. This seemingly declining interest in Canadian affairs could appear rather startling. But remember this was before the 24/7 news cycle and there were a limited number of pages in a daily paper. Communism, with the Cuban missile crisis and the Vietnam War, was just one of the many serious issues emerging in the United States during the mid-twentieth century. This was the beginning of the "space race" with the Soviets' launch of Sputnik, the years when the Little Rock Nine and Dr. Martin Luther King Jr. appealed for racial equality, the years right before President Richard Nixon's declaration of a war on drugs. Policy disagreements with Canada ranked low on the human interest barometer that propels every news story. After all, Canada was America's staunchest ally. Wasn't it?

TRADING WITH THE RED MENACE

In 1951, the *New York Times* sent Richard Parke north of the border to report on Canada's role in the rapidly escalating international conflict pitting democracy against communism. Canada, reported Parke, "is mobilizing her tremendous resources toward becoming a major partner in the collective defense of the Western World."[3] He continued on, saying that Parliament, after some initial hesitation, was debating a three-year, five-million dollar defence program. With a combination of "industrial might" and an abundance of natural resources such as oil, copper, and aluminum, Parke wrote that the country was "ready to repeat her World War II role as an arsenal for democracy."[4] His positive description of Canada highlights a shift in the attitude of the American press after the turn of the century. Gone were the calls for annexation, replaced instead with a grudging respect of Canada's sovereignty.

An early blow to Canada–U.S. relations during the Cold War was the suicide of E. Herbert Norman, Canada's ambassador to Egypt. On 4 April 1957, the veteran diplomat leapt to his death from the eighth floor of the Swedish Minister's residence in Cairo. Norman suggested in two suicide notes that revived accusations of communist ties by the United States Senate Internal Security Subcommittee had led him to jump. The Canadian Parliament was outraged, calling Norman's suicide "murder by slander."[5] The government asked for assurances that any security information given to the United States would not be passed along to Congress unless Ottawa gave its consent. In damage-control mode, President Dwight Eisenhower took advantage of a news conference to speak fondly of the strong ties between the two nations.

Meanwhile the *Washington Post* called for the subcommittee members to apologize. Concerned that the suicide might deteriorate cross-border relations, the paper appealed to the sensibilities of Canadians, which it wrote, "ought to persuade them that it would be calamitous to burn down the bridge between Ottawa and Washington merely because a few beavers have gnawed at the timbers."[6]

At the *New Republic* magazine, Philip Deane waved off fears of potential structural damage to the framework of bilateral comradeship. Nothing within reason, he argued, could harm relations as the progress of both countries depended on the other. Still, he cautioned that the "inevitability of ever closer relations is the main reason why the US should not needlessly offend Canada. The US should act with particular courtesy, not to avert the imaginary danger of losing an uncertain ally, but out of consideration for its staunchest friend."[7] The true depth of that friendship would soon be tested by a change in Canada's leadership.

After twenty-two years of Liberal rule, Canadians gave Conservative leader John Diefenbaker a landslide victory in the 1958 election, handing his party the largest number of seats in Canadian political history. Diefenbaker's election campaign had played to a growing sense of nationalism. That, along with festering dissatisfaction over American policies on trade and Congress' handling of the Herbert Norman tragedy, was placing a northern chill on Canada–U.S. relations.

When the United States imposed an embargo on all exports except food and medicine to Cuba in October 1960, Canada declined to do the same. Instead, Canadian businessmen visited Fidel Castro's communist island to drum up business while Cubans headed to Ottawa asking to buy supplies they'd previously ordered from the United States. The *Chicago Tribune* reported the Cuban government projected a tenfold increase, up to 150 million dollars, in trade between Cuba and Canada the following year.[8] Members of Congress and State Department officials were shocked that a trustworthy ally was stepping in to fill the market gap left by the Americans.[9]

The *Chicago Tribune* was also quick to lambaste Canada for its perceived Judas move. It wrote that after linking hands, it seemed Canada and the United States were walking away in different directions. The paper pointed out that Canada, along with the United States and eighteen European nations, had just signed a treaty founding the Organisation for Economic Co-operation and Development (OECD). We should think, the paper editorialized, that "before launching out on cooperation in the more remote areas of the globe, the Canadians might consider the advisability of a little cooperation with the United States in the containment of conspiratorial activities in this hemisphere."[10]

Canada's trade with Cuba remained a touchy subject. As President John F. Kennedy took office in 1961, the *Los Angeles Times* listed several issues the new president would have to deal with — Cuba, Latin America, and the "slow deterioration of our relations with Canada."[11] A year later, the *Washington Post*'s George Sokolsky wrote that Canada's relations with Cuba made little sense. With reports showing that the 150-million dollar upswing in trade had never materialized, Sokolsky argued that Canada's business dealings with the communist nation weren't large enough to justify losing the United States' friendship. "To most Americans," he wrote, "it looks like spite and spite is cheap, no matter why it is done or by whom."[12] In his view, the Cuban problem had now become a Canadian one. "Canada," Sokolsky argued, "is so absorbed by the absurd notion that a small nation can compete successfully with an enormous nation, such as the United States is, that the United States can be sacrificed for the tenuous possibilities of trade with Cuba and Red China. The Canadians can find themselves out on a limb."[13] Despite American disapproval, the Canadian government resolutely — from the U.S. side it seemed almost defiantly — continued establishing separate trade policies with communist governments.

In September 1963, the Canadian government signed a 500-million dollar wheat deal with the Soviet Union and agreed to send some of the shipments to Cuba. The New Republic noted that this arrangement had a value four times greater than total U.S. trade with the Soviet bloc in 1962.[14] The Canadian Wheat Board negotiated another deal with the USSR in 1966. This time it was an 800-million dollar cash sale — the largest wheat transaction ever.[15] A multi-million dollar wheat deal was also struck with China. How did the Canadian government reconcile its opposition to communism with its support of these trade relationships? As the Los Angeles Times quoted of Canadian External Affairs Minister Paul Martin, the idea was that trade would help "minimize the mischief of isolation."[16]

Other countries agreed with this perspective of engaging communist governments rather than clamping down supplies. When it came to Cuban trade relations, Britain, Italy, Spain, Japan, Sweden, Switzerland, and the Netherlands joined Canada as the top countries conducting regular business with Fidel Castro.[17] In 1964, the Chicago Tribune reported that Britain would be selling at least four hundred buses to Cuba. The Chicago Tribune was incensed by the double-dealing. "This is the latest of a number of deals Castro has made with our allies which are thwarting our policy of trying to isolate Castro and thus bring about his downfall," said the Tribune.[18] Over at the Los Angeles Times, Robert Allen and Paul Scott wrote that, unable to exert control over allied countries slapping together backroom deals, America's "so-called 'economic blockade' against Communist-ruled Cuba is as full of holes as a sieve, and all indications are this farcical situation will continue."[19] And it did.

Three years later, the *Chicago Tribune*'s Ottawa correspondent Eugene Griffin commented that Canada wasn't likely to abandon its trade with communist nations. Still, the paper didn't judge its northern neighbour too harshly. "Perhaps we should not be too disappointed," said the *Tribune*. "Our other so-called allies and the countries of what is called the 'free world' are equally faithless.... So we can't be too disenchanted that Canada's affection is less than complete."[20] But there was more to the waning affections of Canada than differing trade policies. The two countries were also at odds over North American defence.

BOMARCS, NUKES, AND DEFENCE

On 12 May 1958, the United States and Canada formally established NORAD, the North American Air Defense Command (renamed the North American Aerospace Defense Command in 1981). The agreement integrated the countries' air-defence forces through a command headquarters in Colorado Springs, Colorado. The idea was that through this joint partnership, North America (minus Mexico) would become a coordinated shield that detected and deterred air attacks from "the outside" — in the fifties and sixties that meant Soviet attacks launched from Russia or Cuba.

At this point Canada was not a nuclear nation. As Congress debated revising the Atomic Energy Act so that the United States could share nuclear weapons information with Britain, the *New York Times* questioned why Canada had been left out of this discussion. After all, it was now helping protect the continent through NORAD. "Is Canada to be treated as a second-rate military partner in a defense program of vital mutual concern to both of us?" asked the *Times*. "If Britain — by revision of the Atomic Energy Law — is to be strengthened by American atomic arms — as she should be — why not Canada, good neighbor and close friend?"[21] A year later, in May 1959, the issue was resolved with the signing of an agreement that allowed Canada and the United States to exchange information on nuclear weapons and research for mutual defence purposes. From his desk at the *Montreal Star*, G.V. Ferguson wrote in the *Washington Post* that the move further integrated continental defence systems. "The obvious dependence of Canada upon its big neighbor is of course increased," he said. "If future warfare depends on nuclear weapons, Canada will have to depend upon the United States for research, for skills and for the weapons themselves."[22] That statement was already proving true.

In the fall of 1958, Prime Minister John Diefenbaker had announced the Canadian government would build anti-aircraft missile bases in North Bay, Ontario, and La Macaza, Quebec. The United States would supply the Bomarc missiles, but the Canadian government hesitated in asking for the nuclear warheads the missiles could carry. As the government wavered, it appeared its citizens didn't. A Gallup poll in December 1961 found that 61 percent of Canadians approved of their military forces being equipped with nuclear weapons.[23] As with all statistics, figures are relative. One could also argue the flip side that more than a third of Canadians disagreed with the idea. Ultimately, the decision would be put off for a few years and re-emerge as an election issue.

In the meantime, Canada's air defence industry was dealt a severe blow when Diefenbaker announced in February 1959 that his government was axing the famed supersonic Avro Arrow project. The Associated Press reported that Diefenbaker defended the abrupt policy shift by saying the interceptor jet aircraft had become increasingly irrelevant in the new age of missiles.[24] At the *New York Times*, the news story was accompanied by the headline "Canada Abandons Military Jet Plan."[25] The *Times* also printed a two-paragraph Associated Press update quoting Claude Jodoin, president of the Canadian Labour Congress, as saying that at "one stroke, the Canadian aircraft industry has virtually been eliminated and the workers have been told that there is no alternative employment for them."[26]

Filing from Ottawa, the *Chicago Tribune's* Eugene Griffin noted that many Canadians "have been stung to resentment by the fact that in abandoning the Arrow the government is substituting a cheaper, more effective Bomarc ground to air missile made by Boeing in the United States."[27] Griffin wrote

14,000 Idled as Canada Junks Its Jet Program

TORONTO, Feb. 21 (AP)— The Avro Aircraft Co. stood crippled today by a stunning government policy switch. Nearly 14,000 people are without jobs and there are fears the unemployed figure could reach 30,000.

A. V. Roe (Canada) Ltd., shut down its two firms in nearby Malton—Avro Aircraft and Orenda Engines Limited —a few hours after the government dropped its supersonic Arrow jet program yesterday in favor of Bomarc guided missiles manufactured in the United States.

There was no advance notice of the decision, announced to Parliament by Prime Minister John Diefenbaker.

The dismissals at Avro meant a weekly payroll loss of $1 million. Avro suppliers employ another 15,000 persons.

Uproar about the government decision increased by the hour. At least $400 million had been spent on the Arrow program, which Diefenbaker said had to be junked because it ran head on into the missile age.

The Avro Arrow has become immortalized in Canadian history, but at the time of its cancellation, the project's demise received little attention in the American media other than standard wire stories like this one from the Associated Press. (*Washington Post*, 22 February 1959)

that the Avro Arrow's cancellation had sparked fresh calls by Canadians for a "fair share" of American defence orders. "Industries, public officials, unions, and newspapers look to the United States as obliged, as an ally and rich neighbor, to spend millions on defense contracts to create employment in this county," he said.[28]

But Griffin's coverage of the Avro Arrow's demise was a rare read. Other than the standard wire articles and a couple reports written by journalists, the project's cancellation — viewed as a highly controversial move in Canada — caused barely a ripple in the American press. Oddly enough, the *Los Angeles Times* appeared to ignore this story even though its circulation area encompassed Los Angeles County, a hotbed for the nation's aerospace industry.

With NORAD and missile defence now squeezing Canada into a corner when it came to accepting nuclear weapons, G.V. Ferguson wrote in the *Washington Post* that Canadians were wary of compromising their country's sovereignty. "Few fears are more real to Canadians than that of United States control of nuclear or atomic weapons carried on Canadian airplanes or launched from Canadian missile sites," he said. "Canada is anxious to play as full a role as it can but, fearful of atomic war, it wants to make sure that its sovereignty, even under the limitations of joint defense, remains complete."[29]

Balancing the see-saw of Canadian sovereignty on one end and North American defence on the other presented an inherent challenge, particularly during the Cuban missile crisis in October 1962. During this square off between the United States and the USSR, the Canadian government, although worried about how Americans would react to Soviet military buildup in Cuba, pledged to support the U.S. in the crisis. So when American military officials asked permission for a massive increase in flights with nuclear weapons across Canadian territory, they didn't expect a problem, reported syndicated political columnist Marquis Childs.[30] But he wrote that four days passed before Diefenbaker's government sent its reply – and then it only gave permission for a few overflights. Childs noted:

> It would be hard to exaggerate the anger in the Pentagon at this outcome. Both the delay and what appeared as a higgling and almost obstructive response had the look, to those managing the deterrent during what was certainly the gravest crisis since the end of World War II, of deliberate refusal on the part of an ally and nearest neighbor to cooperate in the mutual defense of North America.[31]

The *Chicago Tribune* picked up the story, also reporting that Diefenbaker and his government hesitated in approving NORAD's call to place Canadian forces on a full alert. Even after formally authorizing the action, the *Tribune* wrote that much to the chagrin of the United States, the Canadian government didn't arm its planes and missiles with nuclear warheads or send interceptor jets to northern bases.[32]

Senator Wayne L. Morse, a Democrat from Oregon, later pointed to the Cuban missile crisis as the moment it became clear that the fifty-six Bomarc-B missiles were useless without their nuclear warheads and the sixty-four Voodoo jet interceptors were not nearly as effective without their nuclear rockets. Americans "were made painfully aware that the failure of Canada to make good on her joint defense obligations left a gaping hole in the air defenses of the United States," Morse was quoted as saying in a wire story printed in the *Washington Post*.[33] Faced with what it considered an unacceptable non-uniform approach to continental air defence, the United States pushed for new Canadian defence policies.

On 30 January 1963, the U.S. State Department sent a policy paper to the Canadian embassy in Washington criticizing Canada's delay in accepting nuclear arms. The paper argued that effective defence of North America against Russian bombers depended on both countries having nuclear-capable weapons. Department officials then sent out the policy paper as a press release — not the best public relations move to make with an ally.

Reaction was swift, with Diefenbaker decrying the statement as an intrusion into Canadian affairs. Secretary of State Dean Rusk quickly apologized although he defended his government's actions by saying that the disclosure of confidential information during a parliamentary debate the week before had forced the American government to publicly state its position on the nuclear weapons issue.

Never ones to let silence overrule free speech, it didn't take long for the American papers, ink in hand, to march into the fray with thoughts of their own. At the *Washington Post*, an editorial praised Rusk for his even temper during a press conference addressing Canadian criticisms of the policy paper. "No necessity is more fundamental to our foreign policy than continued amity with a country where a common border and common heritage imposes common sense limitations on contention," wrote the *Post*. "We can afford some distemper in Ottawa; we cannot afford to respond in kind."[34]

The *New York Times* agreed, saying the tough talk had to stop. The State Department's comments were "ill-considered and unusually blunt" wrote the *Times*.[35] And, it added, Diefenbaker's retort that Canada would not be pushed around or treated as a "satellite" to the U.S. seemed to pander to anti-American and anti-nuclear sentiment among some Canadians.[36] Still, despite nasty jabs from both sides of the border, the *Times* remained confident that the situation would simmer down. The "destinies of Canada and the United States are so inextricably intertwined that no temporary disagreement can possibly separate us," it wrote. "As in the case of so many other disputes, this one will also have to be settled in the spirit of the century-old friendship and cooperation that have made American–Canadian relations a model for the world."[37]

Out in Chicago, the *Tribune* placed part of the blame for the fracturing cross-border relations on President Kennedy's administration. Calling the State Department's actions "inept diplomacy," the paper said that though Canada was obviously trying to back out of its NORAD commitments, the administration could have more tactfully expressed its frustrations over the country's continual waffling on nuclear weapons. "Instead, they used a club and invited the Canadian allegation that the United States was attempting to push Canada around and was seeking to impose external domination over Canadian affairs," wrote the *Tribune*.[38]

In California, the *Los Angeles Times*, ever one to buck the trend, defended the State Department's open rebuke of Canadian defence policies. Sure there might have been a more diplomatic way of spurring Canada to accept nuclear weapons instead of "airing out the dirty wash where all can see," wrote the *Times*.[39] But, the paper added, it was "encouraging to note that the United States is finally beginning to stand up and get tough with allies who are willing to accept our help but who won't take the responsibility that goes with that assistance."[40]

For Washington-based political columnist Max Freedman, who had grown up in Winnipeg, Manitoba, and regarded Diefenbaker as a "troublesome and unreliable colleague,"[41] the public slap down of Canadian defence policy served no purpose but to raise issues that would strain bilateral relations. Yet Freedman remained optimistic that arching ideals would prevail over squabbles. "Sometimes Canada and the United

States may be on opposite sides of the conference table but they will always be on the same side of the barricades when peace and freedom are in danger," he wrote in a column carried by the *Washington Post*. "That is the sovereign fact about their relationship."[42] Canada, he argued, was firmly committed to the United States. As the only country neighbouring both the U.S. and the USSR, Canada could have positioned itself as an Arctic Switzerland, maintaining neutrality in the Russian–American race for superiority. Instead it had chosen to side with the United States. Now, Freedman wrote, Canadians found themselves mired in a moral dilemma, "an agony of conscience" as he called it, weighing the pros and cons of arming their military forces with nuclear weapons. He challenged his readers to understand what really drove Canadian policy, particularly the insurgent national sentiment that routinely seemed to dictate government action.

In Canada, the odds of an election were increasing with each passing day as leaders in Ottawa pushed opposite agendas when it came to nuclear weapons. Prime Minister Diefenbaker argued for renegotiation of nuclear arrangements with the United States while opposition Liberal leader and Nobel Peace Prize winner Lester Pearson took the position that Canada should honour its commitments.

On 5 February 1963, a vote of non-confidence by a coalition of opposition parties toppled Diefenbaker's minority government and ended the verbal chaos in the House of Commons. The issue of whether to accept nuclear weapons would be brought directly before the Canadian people. News that another election had been called in Canada, just ten months after the previous one, alarmed the *New York Times*. "The political crisis in Canada could deal another blow to Western and Hemispheric solidarity and even endanger the defense of the North American continent," it wrote.[43]

As he'd done before, Diefenbaker was expected to employ his proven campaign strategy — Canadianism, or as seen by journalists on the other side of the border, the old rallying cry of anti-Americanism. Reporter Harlan Byrne at the *Wall Street Journal* was appalled, reminding readers that "Tweaking Uncle Sam's beard is nothing new for Canadian politicians."[44] But he argued that in this particular election campaign the stakes were high as an anti-American strategy in Diefenbaker's camp could "jeopardize continental defense, Canadian–U.S. friendship, and Canada's economic and political stability."[45]

Of course, the nuclear arms issue was one of serious concern, with the potential to drastically affect long-term relations. But remember similar statements of woe and doomsday scenarios during the 1911 election over free trade? History had since shown that both countries continued to prosper after that agreement failed. So it seemed now that the *Wall Street Journal* and *New York Times*' comments reflected Americans' hurt and anger more than possible trade or defence repercussions.

With Canadians deciding the future direction of their country, Drew Pearson at the *Washington Post* focused on how the United States could firm up a faltering friendship. Using the two countries' intricate defence relationship as an example, Pearson asked why this same kind of interconnectedness couldn't operate in the sphere of governance. Allow two Canadian delegates to sit in Congress, one in the House of Representatives and one in the Senate, he proposed, and in turn send two American delegates to Ottawa, one to each chamber of Parliament. The delegates would participate in deliberations but have no voting privileges. "This may sound like a revolutionary proposal," Pearson wrote. "However these are revolutionary days when it comes to missiles and weapons, and political advance must move fast to keep abreast of the modern technological world."[46] It was a novel idea, one that was not followed up on but nevertheless innovative and worthy of more than a passing glance. The prospect of two delegates attending sessions at each government body, though it could be viewed as compromising sovereignty, potentially addressed two oft-repeated grievances: that of better American understanding of Canadian issues and that of Canada desiring a higher profile south of the border.

As the 1963 election campaign rolled on, both the *Los Angeles Times* and the *Washington Post* carried stories of Diefenbaker promising a cheering hometown crowd in Prince Albert, Saskatchewan, that Canada would not become a "storage dump" for nuclear weapons if he were re-elected.[47] Instead he argued that nuclear weapons be kept in the United States and brought across the border only during a crisis, an arrangement American strategists considered impractical.

By the end of March, with less than two weeks left on the hustings, Harlan Byrne with the *Wall Street Journal* noted that Diefenbaker's campaign hadn't taken an aggressive anti-American stance. The prime minister "so far has been only jabbing rather than slugging at the U.S., which triggered the crisis that brought down his government last month," Byrne wrote from Ottawa.[48] Perhaps Diefenbaker was only jabbing because the backlash would be too great if he slugged. In an article that appeared in the *Los Angeles Times*, Samuel Lubell reported from Toronto that two out of three Canadians he interviewed said they approved of Canada accepting nuclear weapons from the United States.[49] Although a highly unscientific study, Lubell's results mirrored those of the Gallup poll conducted little more than a year before (quoted earlier). Among the people he spoke to, Lubell noticed a divide in opinion about the United States. In particular, he was struck by the level of anti-Americanism. "Like most Americans, I have never thought that the United States has a 'Canadian problem,'" he wrote. "But for some years to come, I suspect Americans will have to learn to adjust to a restless, none-too-satisfied neighbor on our Northern frontier."[50]

On 8 April, Lester Pearson and his Liberal Party won enough seats to form a minority government. Canadians had booted Diefenbaker out. Drew Pearson, in the *Washington Post*, had projected this outcome, writing on the day of the election that the majority of Canadians were anxious not to loosen ties with the United States. He attributed the Liberal win to decades of cooperation on both sides of the border:

> It is not for nothing that Canada and the United States have boasted the longest undefended border in the world. It is not for nothing that we have exercised a minimum of red tape in crossing back and forth to enjoy unique scenery, climate and culture. It is not for nothing that Canadians and Americans have intermarried, attended each other's universities, and worked together in mutual defense. And despite the booboos of Washington, and the twisting of

Washington's mistakes by Diefenbaker, this deep-rooted friendship is coming to the surface.[51]

During the so-called "60 days of decision," when Prime Minister Lester Pearson promised to do more in his first sixty days than any other Canadian government, the Liberals sent a clear signal to ease the snippy, strained dialogue that had developed between Ottawa and Washington. Within weeks of his election as prime minister, Pearson reaffirmed his campaign promise that Canada would accept nuclear weapons from the United States for its military forces at home as well as its NATO forces in Europe. The *New York Times* welcomed the news that Canada's foreign policy was swinging back to a pro-American position. "Mr. Pearson has reversed the basically isolationist and anti-American stance of the Diefenbaker regime in favor of interdependence and cooperation with the United States," it wrote.[52] Note the *Times*' use of the word "regime." In choosing a term that's used to describe oppressive governments (a "military regime" or the "Nazi regime"), it appeared the paper's editorial board couldn't resist one last dig at "Dief the Chief."

A few days later, the *New York Times* printed another editorial heralding Canada's acceptance of nuclear arms and dispensed some advice of its own. "The United States has often regarded Canada as a member of the family and has taken that great nation too much for granted," it said. "More tact and an appreciation on our part of some of the peculiar economic and political difficulties of the Canadians, and a wider understanding on the part of Canada that we stand or fall together, are indispensable prerequisites for the new era that is now hopefully launched."[53]

But this new era in Canada–U.S. relations would struggle to materialize during Pearson's two terms as prime minister. Compounding policy differences on Cuba, the Soviet Union and nuclear weapons, there was also the Vietnam War.

VIETNAM VARIANCE

When it came to the Vietnam War, Canada was officially "non-belligerent," that is, it didn't take part militarily in the war. From 1954 to 1973, Canadian officials served on two international truce commissions and the country supplied millions of dollars of humanitarian aid to South Vietnam. Still, its real role during the war remained nuanced with clandestine as opposed to overt support of American efforts.

Compared to the other diplomatic crises during this volatile period in American–Canadian relations, Canada's role in and opposition to the Vietnam War received the least amount of attention and criticism from the American press. Perhaps this is because American journalists were focused on covering the multitude of war-related stories in their own country. As would occur decades later during the wars in Iraq and Afghanistan, during the Vietnam years the American media rarely reported on other nations (besides the enemy) involved in the conflict. Certainly, the lack of articles seems to indicate scant public awareness of Canada's co-operation with the CIA in espionage or the use of its military bases as a testing ground for "Agent Orange" and carpet-bombing runs. If American journalists had heard any rumours or received any leads, they weren't vigorously chasing them.

Among the American newspapers, the *Chicago Tribune* was extremely vocal in criticizing Canadian policy as well as efforts made to broker peace between Hanoi and Washington. In the early months of 1965, the United States escalated its attacks against communist North Vietnamese leader Ho Chi Minh and his Democratic Republic of Vietnam (DRV). The *Tribune* chastised Prime Minister Lester Pearson for questioning whether the South Vietnamese people supported American war efforts in the region. "Well, thanks," wrote the *Tribune*. "How this kind of chatter helps is beyond us. Canada makes much of being a neighbor with an unguarded frontier, but Canadian leaders spend much of their time undercutting American policy."[54] Drawing on events from the past few years, the paper carried on, saying that first Canada "sabotaged" the embargo with Cuba, and then bailed out the Soviet Union and China with wheat deals, and now it was helping an enemy by taking a swipe at America's attempts to retain freedom in Southeast Asia. "This is the kind of ally in which we can hardly rejoice," the paper harrumphed.[55]

MUDDYING THE WATERS

Events in Viet Nam are confusing enough without the contributions of some gentlemen who are muddying the waters even further. Prime Minister Lester Pearson of Canada, for example, offers the gratuitous observation that our activities in the war there have no solid basis of support among the South Vietnamese themselves.

Mr. Pearson said there is always a strong temptation to tweak the American eagle's tail feathers, and then proceeded to indulge in the sport himself. First warning against "hasty condemnation," he then asked why the South Vietnamese didn't fight their own war. His proposed solution was neutralization of the whole territory, but he conceded that this would lead to communization thru the agency of Red China.

Well, thanks. How this kind of chatter helps is beyond us. Canada makes much of being a neighbor with an unguarded frontier, but Canadian leaders spend much of their time undercutting American policy. It was Canada that took the lead in sabotaging the American trade embargo against Cuba. It was Canada which helped bail Red China and the Soviet Union out of economic distress by initiating huge wheat deals on credit. Now it is the Canadian prime minister who gives aid and comfort to the communist enemy by deriding American attempts to keep islands of freedom in Asia.

This is the kind of ally in which we can hardly rejoice.

———————————————————

In the American press, the *Chicago Tribune* was one of the most outspoken in criticizing Canadian policy during the Vietnam War. (*Chicago Tribune*, 12 February 1965)

By April, Pearson, with Nobel Peace Prize credentials largely defining his reputation, called for a pause in American air strikes to see if that might encourage the start of peace negotiations. Accepting Temple University's World Peace Award on 2 April in Philadelphia, the prime minister was quoted by the Associated Press as saying, "There does appear to be at least a possibility that a pause in such air strikes against North Vietnam at the right time might provide the Hanoi authorities with an opportunity, if they wish to take it, to inject some flexibility into their policy without appearing to do so as the direct result of military pressure."[56] Writing for the *New York Times*, William Weart said Pearson also emphasized he was not "proposing any compromise on points of principle, nor any weakening of resistance to aggression in South Vietnam."[57]

But Pearson's comments may have pushed too hard. Legend goes so far as to say that during a lunch and informal chat at Camp David the next day, President Johnson lost his temper and pinned Pearson against a railing, grabbed him by the collar, and lifted him off the ground, bellowing, "You pissed on my rug!"

What we do know from press reports is that tensions were high that spring day. As journalists crowded around the two men during a press briefing on a terrace outside the presidential lodge, the *Washington Post*'s Laurence Stern observed that Johnson "sat stonily at Pearson's side" while Cabell Phillips commented for the *New York Times* that the president "appeared to be in a sober mood and clearly was not desirous of extending the discussions about Vietnam."[58] Meanwhile, the *Los Angeles Times*' Robert Thompson said Johnson looked irritated and after persistent questioning on his reaction to Pearson's speech, snapped that the prime minister's visit had "nothing to do whatsoever with Vietnam — that was not the purpose of it — or anything else that you could blow up or make look big or dramatic."[59] On the contrary, Thompson noted that both men described their discussion as being "very friendly." "'We have no news for you,' said the President, who was stretched out in the warm sunshine on a redwood chaise lounge," Thompson wrote. "Pearson added that he also did not have much to say."[60] (A month later, Jay Walz would report for the *New York Times* that Pearson admitted there was an argument that day at Camp David.[61])

While the president was publicly mum on Pearson's pitch for a temporary suspension of air strikes, the *Chicago Tribune* was indignant. "If there is anything to this theory, why does not Ho Chi Minh, the communist boss, order his side to take a 'measured pause' instead of bombing the American embassy in Saigon?" asked the paper. "As an adult with an extended view of international relations, Pearson ought to know by now that it is a bad bet to put your trust in communism, whatever paper commitments it may assume."[62]

But Canada was committed to the pursuit of peace. Along with India and Poland, the country had diplomatic representatives on the International Control Commission for Vietnam. Reuters reported Paul Martin Sr., minister for external affairs and the father of future Prime Minister Paul Martin, saying that while Canada recognized the United States' responsibility in Vietnam, it didn't believe military action would solve the problems there.[63] Six weeks after Prime Minister Pearson suggested a pause in bombings, President Johnson did just that – for six days. But the lull failed to kick-start peace talks and air raids resumed. The *New York Times* wrote that some Ottawa officials felt Washington laid the blame for the failed peace effort squarely on Canada by saying it served as a "third-party messenger" to Hanoi.[64] Martin denied any involvement and with rumours swirling that President Johnson was upset with Pearson, diplomatic relations soured.[65]

It didn't help matters a few months later when the White House released a report calling for continued close and candid conversations between Washington and Ottawa, including more "quiet diplomacy." The *New York Times* quoted the report, which stated in an extraordinarily patronizing manner that when talking to the United States, Canadian officials "must have confidence that the practice of quiet diplomacy is not only neighborly and convenient to the United States but that it is in fact more effective than the alternative of raising a row and being unpleasant in public."[66] The underlying "older brother knows best" tone bristled Canadian officials. It seemed an open rebuke of Prime Minister Pearson's public appeal for suspending air raids back in April. While admitting that closer consultations were needed, Canadian authorities didn't necessarily interpret that as meaning they had to keep their voices at a whisper. "Canadians believe they need no lessons from the United States on 'quiet diplomacy,'" wrote an unnamed *Times* correspondent from Ottawa. "But Ottawa thinks it does not always get the attentive ear of Washington when messages are confined to the channels of 'quiet diplomacy.' The Canadian consensus is that 'the United States has too often taken our friendship for granted.'"[67]

Canada's long-simmering frustrations regarding American relations were once again being reflected among its citizens. In Ottawa, *Wall Street Journal* reporter Vermont Royster wrote of escalating anti-Americanism. There was a good deal of emotion in Canada right now, he said, with many Canadians friendly towards the United States while a loud minority – including broadcasters, and university students and faculty – expressed dissatisfaction with a plurality of American issues. "A small example is the fashion of sneering at U.S. culture, from television to novels," he wrote. "Looming somewhat larger is the criticism of U.S. 'capital infiltration' which is supposedly threatening to swallow Canadian business; this provokes serious debate and remains a national issue. But nothing quite stirs an uproar like U.S. military 'adventurism.'"[68]

This adventurism increasingly pushed Canadians to actions of their own. In November 1965, the *Washington Post* and the *Los Angeles Times* printed an article by the *Times*' Harry Trimborn detailing how the Union générale des étudiants du Québec (UGEQ), a 75,000-strong student group in Montreal, was considering a proposal to help American students who had come to Canada seeking to evade the military draft. Also scattered throughout the mid to late sixties were various print articles reporting on the growing number of draft dodgers in Canada.[69] In 1970, the *Christian Science Monitor*'s Lansing Shepard wrote that evaders said they were treated well despite a Gallup poll showing that only 32 percent of Canadians sympathized with their situation.[68] But these stories remained factual and didn't take sides. There were no comments deriding Canada for becoming a haven for the resisters and deserters, which estimated figures have placed between 30,000 and 125,000.[71]

While Americans slinked across the border, Pearson's government continued pursuing its foreign policy objective of initiating peace talks between North Vietnam and the United States. In 1966, the *Los Angeles Times* reported that the United States had endorsed Paul Martin's plan for a new peace proposal through the International Control Commission.[72] A year later, the U.S. State Department released a statement saying that it had studied Martin's four-point proposal and remarked that it held "considerable promise" in de-escalating the conflict.[73]

As Canada pressed for peace, it was also stocking the American war machine. This dichotomy was too great for *Los Angeles Times* reporter Harry Trimborn to ignore. Paul Martin had told the House of Commons that Canada was "striving to play the honest broker between the combatants," he wrote, but the government "sees no inconsistency between this policy and the fact that Canadian companies earned $260 million in 1965 by making military equipment, ranging from green berets to airplanes, for the U.S. war effort in

Vietnam."[74] With the unemployment rate at record low levels and the GDP rising 6 percent yearly, Canada's domestic agenda was clashing with its foreign policy. Yet the country was largely able to keep the two objectives separate and benefited economically from the war while maintaining its polished peacekeeper image.

At times though, the line between foreign and domestic policy blurred. In 1967, the United States cancelled a contract with Canadian defence suppliers because it couldn't guarantee Pearson's government that the smoke bombs would not be used in Vietnam. Further complicating matters, the Canadian government stipulated that defence products made in the country couldn't be shipped directly to the war zone but instead had to pass through the United States. These conditions reinforced the *Chicago Tribune*'s view that its northern neighbour was shirking the duties expected of an ally. "It is a little different these days from before and during the early days of World War II, when Britain and Canada came running to the United States for protection and were glad to get all the arms America could supply and to pool defense production," wrote the *Tribune*. "But, then, gratitude is notoriously short-lived."[75]

In the midst of continuing turmoil in Vietnam, Canada celebrated its centennial year in 1967. The

UNHELPFUL ALLIES

The United States has been obliged to cancel a defense contract with Canadian defense suppliers for smoke bombs, used to mark targets in combat, rather than yield to the insistence of Prime Minister Pearson's government that they not be used in Viet Nam. The Johnson administration, however, accepted a stipulation that no defense materials made for the United States may be shipped to the war zone directly from Canada, but must be transshipped thru the United States.

Pearson's reluctance to support American intervention in Viet Nam may have something to do with Canadian sales of wheat to the Soviet Union and Red China, tho American defense spending in Canada funnels more hard currency to that country than any sales to communist nations. On the other hand, the prime minister may sympathize with the Viet Cong and North Viet Nam and feel that Americans are abusing them.

It is a little different these days from before and during the early days of World War II, when Britain and Canada came running to the United States for protection and were glad to get all the arms America could supply and to pool defense production. But, then, gratitude is notoriously short-lived.

Another reaction from the *Chicago Tribune* regarding Canadian government policy positions during the Vietnam War. (*Chicago Tribune*, 3 March 1967)

New York Times and *Washington Post* took note of the big birthday bash. Calling it a year of soul-searching, Jay Walz with the *Times* wondered, "Does the future hold true nationhood for this land of remarkable opportunity and potential wealth? Or will an accumulation of tensions and embittering disputes tear it apart, a development that some Canadian political scientists believe would be but a prelude to absorption by the United States."[76] Walz wrote that sharp foreign policy differences on Vietnam, Cuba and other communist nations as well as disputes with the U.S. over water and investment capital in Canada could be indicative of two things — either Canada's problems or its increasing national prominence. At no time in its history has Canada "been more divided over her proper course, more uneasy about 'Canadianism,' and more tense about relations with her southern neighbor than she is at the outset of this national celebration," said Walz.[77]

Marquis Childs had a different view of Canada's status as it celebrated its first one hundred years. "In Canada's long search for nationhood — for identity — the birthday party is a way of saying, 'Look, we're a hundred years old, we're grown-up now. And anyone who talks about our becoming the 51st state of the United States had better duck quick,'" he wrote.[78] As Walz had done, Childs commented on the cyclopean amount of American funds heading north. He wrote that as much as 30 percent of all Canadian capital investment was now coming from the United States, with Americans supplying 80 percent of the financing for the expansive development of resources such as oil, minerals, and natural gas. "The need for this flow helps to explain Canada's fear — some would say neurotic fear — of domination by her only neighbor, the most powerful nation in the world," said Childs. "While the partnership symbolized by the longest undefended border, to use the favorite cliche, is essential, it is nevertheless subject to constant pinpricks of resentment."[79]

Lester Pearson was Canada's prime minister for five years. When he left, the "pinpricks" would become persistent pokes. For in 1968, Trudeaumania struck.

CHAPTER 4

ENTER THE INTELLECT

1968–1984

Even if the two nations succeed in patching up their disagreements in the coming months, it may well be that they are destined to grow further apart. ~ *Claude Lemelin, Editor, Le Devoir de Montréal, 24 October 1971*

If I were president of the United States, every morning I would thank God that I had Canada as a neighbour. ~ *Brian Mulroney, Opposition Leader, Conservative Party, 1 May 1984*

Pierre Elliott Trudeau. Depending on who you are, that name evokes different reactions. A young Canadian will know of Trudeau as the prime minister who patriated the Constitution. But those who remember the "Trudeau years" know of a multi-dimensional man, a leader of complexity whose policies fascinated yet alienated both Canadians and Americans. For there is no one way to define Trudeau — to do so would be an insult to his intelligence. He was the swinging bachelor and a family man, a devout Catholic and supporter of abortion and homosexuality, a politician who based his legacy on separation from Britain and fought those same desires when they came from Quebec.

Flamboyant yet subdued, Pierre Trudeau was a darling — and frequently a target — of the media. In the United States, the American press devoted an unprecedented amount of coverage to this 15th prime minister of Canada. There were stories about his personality, policies, and love life. Unable to ignore Trudeau as it had other prime ministers, America's attention fixed northward, up to the continent's "attic" where the boxes of Canadian politics and standard procedure were being shuffled in the frenzy of spring cleaning.

TRUDEAUMANIA

A neophyte in the copper-gilded world of rules and established decorum, Pierre Trudeau had been a member of Parliament for just three years when he was persuaded to run for the Liberal Party leadership in April 1968 as Prime Minister Lester Pearson was retiring. The mere announcement that the law professor-turned politician-turned justice minister was entering the scuffle of party convention politics caught the attention of the American media. It seemed the 46-year-old (journalists later found out his campaign team had lied and he was two years older) bachelor's freewheeling reputation as an avid fan of sports cars and beautiful blondes had preceded him. "A 'swinging' prime minister for staid old Canada?" asked the *Wall Street Journal*'s Robert Prinsky.[1]

Over at the *Washington Post*, foreign correspondent Robert Estabrook wrote from Ottawa that Trudeau was the "most dazzling" of the nine contestants for the Liberal leadership and the "most exciting phenomenon in Canada since Expo 67."[2] The *New Republic* magazine was less effusive but equally imaginative, with writer Alex Campbell describing Trudeau as a "go-go French Canadian so cool he dispenses with a top coat whenever Ottawa's winter temperature soars to 12 degrees."[3] (The presumption is that Campbell was referring to degrees Fahrenheit.)

But the millionaire in Carnaby Street clothes was raising eyebrows in another way. American papers wrote of Trudeau's background that included studies at Harvard and the London School of Economics, trips to communist countries such as the Soviet Union and China, and a reported admiration of far left-leaning socialist values, which had led to him being barred from entering the United States in the 1950s. "He is not at all the man the CIA or the State Department would pick to be prime minister of America's Northern neighbor," wrote Campbell. "If he succeeds Pearson there will be sleepless nights in Maclean,

Virginia, and in Foggy Bottom."[4] Only government officials in Washington know whether their sleeping patterns changed the night of 5 April when Trudeau, during an emotional and chaotic convention, was elected the Liberal Party's new leader on the fourth ballot. The man who had called Prime Minister Pearson and his Liberals "idiots" for accepting nuclear weapons from the United States was now that party's leader. Four days after being sworn in as prime minister on 20 April, Trudeau called a snap election for June. He was banking on momentum and a country that was ready for change to give his party a majority of seats in the House of Commons.

It seemed Trudeau had nothing to lose and all to gain in this election for it quickly became apparent that he was able to grasp hold of an intangible asset — the imaginations of Canadians. At the *Washington Post*, editors reprinted an article from the Chicago Daily News Service's Frank Flaherty in Ottawa. Under the headline "Trudeau: Monsieur Playboy," Flaherty wrote that this "unusual meteor streaking across Canada's political horizon has a magic that has attracted support from major newspapers as well as younger voters and the academic community."[5]

Trudeaumania was in full swing.

With his blue Mercedes sports car, brown belt in karate, duelling scar on his face, and penchant for arriving at government meetings in sandals, Trudeau appealed particularly to young voters. The *New York Times*' Jay Walz in Ottawa wrote of blonde girls in miniskirts crowding around the prime minister and begging for kisses, of cheering crowds waiting for Trudeau as he arrived and left the Parliament Buildings.[6] An article in the *Times* written by the *Globe and Mail*'s George Bain spoke of the smooching phenomenon. "There is no tradition in Canadian politics even of baby-kissing, and the suggestion that nubile maidens could take to hurling themselves at the neck of the Prime Minister — any Prime Minister that ever was or was likely to be — would have been considered laughable a short time ago," he wrote.[7] This was not the kind of political campaign Americans were used to seeing across the border. Even Bain admitted that, saying "The trait of moderation which is supposed to mark the national character makes positively bizarre the way that any Canadians — especially the young — have been carrying on about him since."[8]

At the *Chicago Tribune*, Trudeau was declared "Canada's version of the Kennedys" with a youth, wealth, and vigour paralleling that of that famed American political dynasty.[9] "Like the Kennedys," the paper wrote, "he regards himself as a pragmatist, which his opponents can easily translate to mean an opportunist."[10] Whether he was taking a pragmatic or opportunistic approach, Trudeau campaigned on the theme "One Canada, One People." The strategy worked. On 25 June, the *New York Times* reported that a record number of Canadians headed to the polls.[11] "Canada," said the *Times*, "has opted for change within a strong federation and has given an intelligent young Prime Minister a stable majority and a clear run of five years to bring it about."[12]

For *Washington Post* reporter Richard Homan, the election results revealed a sudden taste for pop politics among the Canadian public. Voters had embraced a decidedly unconventional prime minister. Here was a leader who once when walking on stage for a national television interview had acknowledged the cheering audience by putting two fingers in his mouth and sending out a shrill whistle.[13] And another time, when asked what he'd do with his Mercedes if he became prime minister, had replied, "Are you now asking about the car or the girl? No matter, I am keeping both."[14]

"After a Kennedy-style campaign that brought the word charisma across the border into Canadian vocabulary and teeny boppers squealing into the streets, Prime Minister Pierre Elliott Trudeau and his Liberal Party have been re-elected to a full term," wrote Homan.[15]

In the *Los Angeles Times*, Max Lerner extrapolated a deeper meaning behind Trudeau's win. At certain times in history, he wrote, people turn to charismatic leaders to reassure themselves of who they are as old beliefs and traditions disappear. With the rise of Trudeaumania, Canada had become a reflection of a larger trend that was affecting Britain and the United States. "The old rituals of our society have broken down," Lerner said, "and to buss a swinger prime minister and dance with him may well be a form of ritual replacement for our time."[16] Canadians had discovered a new national consciousness through Trudeau. The prime minister was shaking things up — and it was more than the booties of miniskirted maidens.

THE SHAKEDOWN

As prime minister, Pierre Trudeau made it clear that he was there to steer Canada on a different course. Some of his policies would later be called the "Third Option," one that would lessen the country's dependence on the United States by establishing stronger trade ties with other nations. This would not be the kind of welcoming message Americans were looking for in the new prime minister. Almost a year after his election win, Trudeau headed south for a 37-hour visit to Washington. The *Washington Post*'s Dorothy McCardle prepared Washingtonians for the unpredictable. "The 49-year-old 'PM,' as the Canadians call him, has a taste for impromptu high jinks, milk, overshoes and pretty girls," she wrote. "He has been known to punctuate a boring party by standing on his head. He has made a grand diplomatic entrance by sliding down the bannisters or vaulting a hand rail."[17]

But the leader who had charmed Canada didn't have the panache it took to wow celebrity-saturated America. The *Washington Post*'s Margaret Crimmins quoted various reactions from bystanders and guests who noted that Trudeau needed a hairpiece, walked pigeon-toed, looked like an elf, and appeared scared when he met President Richard Nixon. When it came to fashion, the prime minister had trouble impressing the ladies as a dashing figure with his tan coat and grey suit. But as the visit wore on, Crimmins wrote that Canada's most eligible bachelor "did seem to get over some of that initial outward shyness which makes him walk like he's going to disappear and brings out the tiny, elf-making veins over his eyes."[18]

Not surprisingly, Trudeau also failed to impress Americans with his plans, especially when he announced during a speech at the National Press Club that Canada would be pursuing friendly but independent policies from those of the United States. This news irritated the *Los Angeles Times*. Of course, the paper said,

Canada and the United States were free to criticize each other and have disagreements. Yet the *Times* warned its northern ally to remember that independence worked both ways. "As a good neighbor, the United States is obligated to consult with our Canadian friends," it wrote. "But as a power with global responsibilities, we need not feel obliged to take their advice – on China, the anti-ballistic missile or anything else."[19]

New policy differences weren't the only annoyances. Trudeau was also tampering with old ones. While in Washington, the prime minister informed President Nixon that the Canadian government would decide shortly whether it would remain a member of the North Atlantic Treaty Organization (NATO). Trudeau had called for a review of Canada's foreign policy and was debating the issue; the NATO charter permitted members to withdraw after twenty years if the country gave twelve months' notice. The *New York Times* was puzzled by the prime minister's stance on a standard defence position. While "the conviction remains here that the Canadians will stay in NATO, the doubt remains," wrote *Times* journalist James Reston. "After all, if you ask the girl if she loves you, and she says, 'I'll think about it and tell you later,' you are bound to wonder if everything's all right."[20] A week and a half after his visit to Washington, Trudeau announced Canada would reduce its military force in Europe but stay in the alliance.

That decision rankled Eugene Griffin, the *Chicago Tribune*'s foreign correspondent. Griffin had been reporting from Canada for twenty-three years, the longest time of any American journalist who had been assigned there. After a tour to the Western provinces in 1969, he wrote from Vancouver that self-interest now propelled Canada's foreign policy decisions, its outlook, and its view of the United States. Griffin was less than pleased with this unilateral approach to a bilateral relationship. "The United States consistently yields to Canada on any question, gives Canada the privileges of more than an ally – as in access to American defense contracts – and respects every inch of Canadian sovereignty, but it remains Canada's favorite whipping boy," he stated in a front-page article.[21]

The whipping was about to get a lot worse. With Americans in control of more than half of Canada's manufacturing, oil refining, and mining industries, there was mounting debate in the country over the extent of American interest in Canadian industries. In January 1970, Trudeau was forced to assure the House of Commons that any deal to sell more oil to the United States wouldn't include handing over the country's water resources or its Arctic sovereignty.[22]

By spring, tensions were blanketing diplomatic discourse like heavy dew. The United States was annoyed at Canada for harbouring draft dodgers, and limiting foreign ownership in uranium mines and possibly other industries. In Ottawa, Canadian officials expressed frustration over several issues – the United States' plan to send the tanker *Manhattan* back to Arctic waters, American determination to place anti-ballistic missiles near the Canadian border and hold nuclear tests in the Aleutian islands, and Nixon's decision to cut Canadian oil imports by a third for the rest of the year. "In view of the many strains that have developed in Canadian–U.S. relations, and the prospect on new ones," wrote Peter Thomson at the *Los Angeles Times*, "some observers feel it is somehow symbolic of the times that U.S. customs officials are now armed."[23]

Canadians' love affair with Trudeau was also taking a hit. In Ottawa, the *New York Times*' Jay Walz found that halfway through Trudeau's first term, the prime minister had failed to deliver on his "Just Society" promises of cultural equality and economic opportunities. "After 24 months the man whom a majority of the voters chose as the leader best qualified to move Canada to new social frontiers finds himself grappling with problems of the old order," wrote Walz. "No sweeping reforms have emerged and Mr. Trudeau is being viewed here less as a visionary than as a disciplinarian teacher who became principal of the school."[24]

A few months later, Trudeau rapped the ruler hard on Quebec.

TRUDEAU AND THE TERRORISTS

On 5 October 1970, the Front de Libération du Québec kidnapped British trade commissioner James Cross. The FLQ, a terrorist group promoting Quebec's independence from Canada, had been responsible throughout the past several years for more than two hundred bombings in places including McGill University and the Montreal Stock Exchange. But the kidnapping of Cross and, a few days later, that of Quebec's labour minister, Pierre Laporte, would force Trudeau to get tough. On 16 October, the prime minister invoked the *War Measures Act*, suspending civil liberties in Quebec and across the country. Laporte's strangled body was found the next day in the trunk of a car near the Saint-Hubert airport, a few kilometres from Montreal.

With the backing of the *War Measures Act*, police arrested hundreds of suspects. In Montreal alone, several thousand troops protected government buildings and public officials. The city was in crackdown and the *Chicago Tribune* applauded the harsh measures:

> Dynamite bombs, murder, and kidnapping for ransom are hallmarks of the revolutionary wherever he is found. He must be faced with the full power of the society he would destroy. As Trudeau said, when he first ordered federal troops to Montreal, "society must take every means at its disposal to defend itself," regardless of the "weak-kneed bleeding hearts." Canada has acted forcefully in this crisis.[25]

Across the border, where Americans were dealing with the crimson stains of urban riots, the assassinations of Dr. Martin Luther King Jr. and Malcolm X, and the potential for more civil unrest, the big question among journalists was whether the federal government could ever impose the same kind of restrictive measures. White House press secretary Ronald Ziegler was quick to remind reporters that the president's emergency powers were limited by the Constitution and it would be up to Congress to call on the militia and suspend the right of habeas corpus.[26]

By the end of October, the *Chicago Tribune*'s Eugene Griffin in Ottawa reported that Trudeau's bold gamble to invoke the *War Measures Act* was paying off. "Prime Minister Pierre Trudeau, the province of Quebec and the Canadian nation have emerged with new strength from terrorist threats to democracy here in the last three weeks," he wrote. "The prime minister is seen today by political observers as a leader who has giant stature on the Canadian if not the world scene."[27]

The *Christian Science Monitor* agreed with Griffin. In an era of rising political terrorism around the world, it wrote that Trudeau's decisive action showed democratic countries how to deal with similar threats. "Canada is no military regime," it said. "It is a democracy that, under Pierre Trudeau, has shown that it knows how to defend itself against the 'radical chic' of political terrorism. Other countries can take notice, and be ready to apply the same courage."[28]

It would take Canadian police officers until December to make their final arrests and negotiate the release of James Cross through an agreement that allowed five FLQ members to be flown to exile in Cuba. With Canada's October Crisis over, it was simply a matter of time before old animosities rose again between Canada and the United States.

BACK TO THE BASICS

In mid-August 1971, President Nixon floated the U.S. dollar, imposed a 10 percent surtax on most imports, and proposed new investment tax credit legislation. The "Nixon Shock" infuriated Canada and Prime Minister Pierre Trudeau didn't shy away from telling the situation as he saw it. In 1970, Canada had exported 10.2 billion dollars of goods to the United States, or to put it another way, 68 percent of the country's total exports had headed south to the land of Stars and Stripes.[29] If the import surcharge insinuated that the United States wanted to buy Canada's natural resources but not its manufactured goods, well, tough policies could go both ways. "I don't think that the United States is deliberately trying to beggar its neighbors and make this into a permanent policy," a United Press International wire story quoted Trudeau as saying during a CBC television interview. "But if it is, we'll have to make a fundamental reassessment of our whole economy."[30] The comment was picked up and reprinted from New York to Chicago and Los Angeles. At the *Los Angeles Times*, associate editor James Bassett wrote, "For the usually soft-spoken Trudeau, nicknamed 'The Shrugger' by his foes because of his reluctance to make direct replies during the

Parliamentary question period, these are fighting words."[31] In apparent retaliation, the Trudeau government cancelled discussions with the United States over joint use of the continent's energy resources.[32]

Inaccurate information and subtle rubs worsened the situation. At a news conference in September 1971, President Nixon was quoted saying that Japan was America's "biggest customer in the world and we are their biggest customer in the world."[33] The facts showed — and Canadians were more than aware — that Canada was the United States' largest trading partner. It also didn't help matters when a top diplomat told journalists that Canadians had become too reliant on American investment and were "hewers of wood and drawers of water because that is what they want to be."[34] In Canada covering Soviet Premier Alexei Kosygin's visit, *Los Angeles Times* staff writer Murray Seeger said statements like these simply served to irritate Canadians further. In an ironic twist on Seeger's comments, a copy editor had written the following headline for his story: "Canada: Rumblings from '51st State' Grow Louder." Even in the newsroom, it seemed the pestering continued, spurred on by the unrelenting push for sales.

Adding further insult to bilateral dialogue, Ottawa was being told that Washington would not make an exception and exclude Canadian goods from the import surcharge. Again, Seeger provided a Canadian perspective on this issue for *Times* readers. "Canada is asking simply to be understood as a sovereign country with its own complex personality," he wrote from Vancouver. "It is a spirited, democratic melting pot demanding recognition on its own terms, but Washington does not seem to be listening."[35]

The *New York Times* called this rocky patch during the Trudeau–Nixon years a low point in cross-border relations. While the paper said Canadian resentment over being ignored or taken for granted by the United States was an old grievance, it was still legitimate. "These American habits long antedate the Nixon Administration, but they become more serious at a time of growing nationalism everywhere," wrote the *Times*. "What the noises from Canada clearly indicate is that the cost of traditional neglect is escalating dangerously."[36]

In Ottawa, *New York Times* correspondent James Reston viewed the situation in more *risqué* terms. Canada, he said, was like a woman having an affair with the wealthy next-door neighbour. While he gave her everything she needed, he had a wandering eye and a lot of other affairs on the go. And therein lay the problem. "It's not the big guy's money she minds," wrote Reston, "but his 'benign neglect,' and like most women, she wants to know 'where all this is leading' and what the big guy's intentions really are."[37]

MacIntosh in the Dayton Journal Herald

"You know, Prime Minister Trudeau, some people think —put my bags over there—that America takes advantage of Canada."

An editorial cartoon pokes fun at Canadian angst over American "domination" of the country's culture and economy as President Richard Nixon visited Ottawa in 1972. (Originally published in the *Dayton Journal Herald;* reprinted in the *Washington Post,* 23 April 1972)

By the time Nixon headed to Ottawa in the spring of 1972, the surcharge had been lifted and journalists saw the visit as an opportunity for the president to assuage Canadian fears of American domination. Indeed, in a nationally televised speech before a joint session of Parliament, Nixon emphasized the need for independence, calling for a new bilateral relationship that recognized the two nations' "separate identities" and the "significant differences" between them.[38] But the *Wall Street Journal* reported there was little the president could do to alleviate Canadian angst over a cultural identity that was seemingly being washed away by a red, white, and blue tide of TV shows, music, and literature. Coming to terms with the unavoidable American cultural saturation would take time, but eventually wrote the *Journal*, "Canadians will successfully pass through this period of cultural trauma — realizing they can eat fried chicken every day for breakfast, work for General Motors of Canada Ltd., queue for 'The Godfather,' and still be distinctly Canadian."[39] Decades later in the twenty-first century, despite Tim Hortons coffee, Canadian Tire, and *Corner Gas*, the "cultural trauma" continues and the *Journal*'s confident prediction seems to have become more resigned fact than embraced reality.

By the mid-seventies, with Trudeau still at the helm of the Canadian federal government, the country's nationalistic agenda was increasingly aggravating bilateral relations. There were new foreign publication rules, price increases in oil exports, and the Saskatchewan government's threat to

Petulant Pierre

Mr. Nixon seems to be taking the fuel shortage in better grace than Canada's Prime Minister Pierre Trudeau.

When his countrymen are being urged to save fuel, Mr. Trudeau continues to ride to work in an armor plated vehicle that appears to use only slightly less gasoline than a battleship. Reporters asked if he planned to switch to a more economical mode of transportation, and Mr. Trudeau replied: "I'll drive a locomotive if I want to."

Of course a head of government should not be expected to ride to work in a car pool. Questions that ignore this reality are either stupid or asked with ulterior and unfriendly motives.

But Mr. Trudeau's petulant response reflects an acerbity ill becoming a prime minister in a period of austerity. It is reminiscent of Marie Antoinette's suggestion that everybody eat cake. It is as if the Canadian leader were saying of his bus-riding critics, "Let 'em drink kerosene."

Initial enthusiasm in the American press for Prime Minister Pierre Trudeau gave way to harsh criticism as the years wore on. (*Chicago Tribune*, 28 December 1973) take over the province's potash industry. Canadians "are suffering an especially intense bout of their peculiarly defensive nationalism," wrote George Will in the *Washington Post*.[40] These new measures were the result of a search he said, for the Canadian soul. But Will argued that exiling American interests wouldn't solve any problems if the country's soul were weak. "Canadian nationalists have a healthy hankering for a national identity," he stated. "But too often they have nothing to say about 'Canadianness'– nothing except a petulant insistence that it means 'not made in the U.S.'"[41] With the Canadian–American relationship in shambles, Trudeau headed to Cuba.

VIVA CUBA!

To the press in the United States, some of Prime Minister Trudeau's actions before he entered federal politics appeared to swerve far left of the American ideal, with travels to communist nations and subscriptions to socialist publications. At the *Chicago Tribune*, Eugene Griffin noted that in an article for the 1961 book, *Social Purpose for Canada*, Trudeau had called for "greater flexibility in the socialist approach to problems of federalism" and lauded China's Mao Tse-tung as a "superb strategist."[42] Once he became prime minister, Trudeau further cemented broad American opinion that he had socialist leanings by establishing diplomatic relations with China and continuing trade with Cuba. In early January 1976, Trudeau went one step further, declaring that the free-market system had failed and calling instead for increased government intervention in the economy.[43] That was too much for many Canadians who roundly criticized the prime minister for his

Prime Minister Pierre Trudeau's chummy relations with Cuba provided inspiration for this editorial cartoon drawn by Peter Kuch at the *Winnipeg Free Press* and reprinted in the *National Review* in 1976.

comments. But that didn't stop Trudeau from squeezing in a quick visit to Cuba a few weeks later while on an official trip to Mexico and Venezuela.

Some in the American press were less than thrilled with this social *tête-à-tête*. The *New York Times* chastised Trudeau for supporting Cuba's involvement with the Soviet Union in Africa. The paper wrote of the prime minister openly praising Fidel Castro as "a man of world stature" who had only sent troops to fight in Angola's civil war after "a great deal of thought and feeling for the situation."[44] "It seems a pity that Prime Minister Trudeau will be unable to extend his goodwill trip to Angola," smirked the *Times*.[45]

At the *Chicago Tribune*, which reported Trudeau as being "positively starry-eyed" during his island visit, an editorial mocked the prime minister's claim that he had gained an understanding of the Angola crisis after talking with Castro:

> We suppose the Socialist point of view justifies invading some one else's country and knocking off people who stubbornly hold a democratic point of view. As we recall, Mr. Trudeau never had much favorable to say when the United States went into Viet Nam to help a government and people who shared *our* point of view. We wish Mr. Trudeau would define for us when noble assistance becomes vicious intervention.[46]

From Ottawa, the *Washington Post*'s Robert Lewis wrote that Trudeau's visit and "particularly his celebrated cry of 'Viva Castro' at a Cuban rally during his tour, drew criticism that he was cuddling with Communism or, at best, sunning himself abroad while preaching restraint at home."[47] Almost a decade after first being elected prime minister, Trudeau's renowned charisma was wearing thin. And the situation would get worse.

BOOTED OUT

In the fall of 1978, with an election expected in the spring, Pierre Trudeau found himself in a political quagmire. While relations with the United States had improved under the administrations of Presidents Gerald Ford and Jimmy Carter, Trudeau's relationship with Canadians had soured. Canada's economy was in a slump with a weak dollar, rapid inflation, and an unemployment rate that was nearly at a post-Depression high. "Just as he was adored as a glamorous young symbol of hope in the 'Trudeaumania' years from 1968 onward, today Trudeau at 59 seems to have become the symbol of Canada's troubles," wrote Ysabel Trujillo, the *Chicago Tribune*'s correspondent for Canada and Latin America. "And he's getting the blame for them."[48]

A few months earlier, the *Wall Street Journal* had questioned Trudeau's policies of wage and price controls. "Mr. Trudeau is whistling in the dark when he voices unconcern," it wrote. "Surely, he must be starting to have some doubts about that theory, which seems to beguile so many national leaders, that a weak currency yields trade benefits."[49] The American press, which had been so intrigued by Trudeau at first, was now clearly tiring of him. Writing from Ottawa for the *Los Angeles Times*, Canada correspondent Stanley Meisler couldn't resist comparing Trudeau to that of a fading Hollywood star. "He seemed more like a movie hero than a politician and his supporters more like adulators than voters," Meisler said. "Since then, Trudeau's achievements have never matched the exaggerated promise of his style."[50]

It seemed in other ways that the prime minister had been around for too long. The dashing bachelor had become a family man, marrying Margaret Sinclair, a 22-year-old self-described "flower child," in 1971. Six years later, he was the separated father of three boys. In his public and private roles, Trudeau had matured and grown older along with his teenybopper supporters — and no one likes to see their aging self reflected in a leader. When the ballot results were tallied on 22 May 1979, the Conservative Party, under Joe Clark's leadership, secured a minority government, ending sixteen years of Liberal rule.

"Au revoir, Pierre" said a headline in the *Chicago Tribune* when Trudeau announced he was stepping down as his party's leader. "Pierre Trudeau, no longer young and no longer a winner," wrote the *Tribune*, saying that after a dramatic career the prime minister's public and private lives had fallen into disorder.[51] "He had to go," stated the paper without a hint of tearfulness.

THE CLARK SIDESHOW

Under Joe Clark's leadership, the Conservatives lasted little more than six months before being tossed out after a vote of non-confidence in the House of Commons. But as prime minister, Clark earned something that had largely proved elusive for Trudeau since the October Crisis in 1970 – accolades from the American press. On 4 November 1979, Iranian student militants stormed the U.S. embassy in Tehran and took sixty-six hostages. In the midst of the chaos, five American diplomats who were at the back of the compound managed to escape undetected. A sixth American working as an agricultural attaché at an office off site also avoided capture. Within days, the diplomats sought sanctuary at the Canadian embassy and spent the next three months sequestered in various staff residences, reading and playing endless games of Scrabble.[52]

But Canadian officials feared it was only a matter of time before their "house guests" would raise suspicions. Complicating matters, several journalists, whose interest had been piqued by witness accounts, discrepancies in the number of hostages held at the U.S. embassy, and the American government's refusal to release a list of those hostages, knew about the clandestine refuge. Although they had honoured Canadian and American government requests to suppress the story, eventually it would break. So in late January 1980, as Iranians were preoccupied with the results of their first presidential election, Canadian embassy officials carried out the "Canadian Caper," sneaking the six diplomats past airport customs officials and out of Iran using fake Canadian passports and forged Iranian visas – all under the guise of shutting down the embassy.

In the American press, Canada's bold covert operation was a top news story nationwide, with the Canadian government receiving immediate respect and praise. "How often do you pick up the paper, read a story about a foreign country, and say to yourself, 'Now *there* is an ally'?" enthused the *Washington Post*.[53] Under the headline "O, Canada!" the *Post* editorial continued, "It was not simply that it was an exceedingly slick and well-executed operation, one worth its own thriller. It was that a friendly nation, at no small risk to its own interests as conventionally conceived, went way out on a limb for an ally and did something truly selfless and honorable."[54]

As Iran's foreign minister condemned the escape and warned of retaliatory measures against Canada and the fifty-three hostages still held at the U.S. embassy, the *Christian Science Monitor* noted, "Canada may have incurred the wrath of Sadeq Ghotbzadeh, but it has won new smiles from the United States of America."[55] After all, it said, this wasn't "the kind of criminal caper Hollywood usually glorifies or the kind of jaunty caper brought to mind when Lawrence Welk plays 'Canadian Capers.' It was a new sort of Canadian caper, and one to be saluted."[56]

And salute Canada Americans did. The Canadian embassy and consulates were flooded with thousands of letters, telegrams, and phone calls; bottles of champagne; boxes of cookies; maple leaf themed cakes — even a marriage proposal from a man claiming to have a Ph.D. and saying he had nothing better to give than himself. Consulate staff in Los Angeles declined that offer.[57] "Suddenly, for thousands of Americans, Canada is a hero,"

U.S. State Department employees carry signs thanking Canada after the Canadian government helps six American diplomats escape from Iran in 1980. News of the "Canadian Caper" inspired spontaneous celebrations and heartfelt gestures of appreciation across the United States. (United Press International)

observed David Andelman at the *New York Times*. "The reaction in the United States has been one of euphoria. State legislatures and colleges are flying maple leaf flags, disc jockeys are composing jingles, tourists are revamping vacation plans, and boards of trade are sponsoring 'Canada Week.'"[58]

In Los Angeles, Mayor Tom Bradley ordered that the Canadian flag be flown at City Hall and declared February "Thank You, Canada, Month" while in New York City, Mayor Ed Koch offered the key to the city to Kenneth Taylor, Canada's (now former) ambassador to Iran who had shepherded the hostages out of the country.[59] President Jimmy Carter phoned Prime Minister Joe Clark to extend a personal thanks and Congress voted to mint a special gold medal for Taylor. "As far as many Americans are concerned, Canada has become the United States' Siamese twin, connected at the heart," wrote *Los Angeles Times* reporter Charles Carney.[60]

At the *Chicago Tribune*, Mary McGrory declared it was time to write an ode to Canada, with an opening line that said the United States was sorry for its condescending attitude. "If Canada were a person," McGrory wrote, "it would probably be a retired nanny or a maiden aunt — someone who lives upstairs in our continent and is never consulted on family affairs but expected to suffer in silence all the thumping and roarings of our family quarrels — and sometimes to deal with the consequences."[61] Now, McGrory said, the Canadians were proving they were the United States' most reliable ally and as such, they deserved more than a nod in appreciation. "Maybe we should invite them to come down from their second-floor room and join us at the table," she cheekily concluded. "We should ask them to share more than the repercussions from our air-traffic jams and our multinational corporations. We should, plainly, ask their opinion."[62]

The *Wall Street Journal* also advocated for a renewed respect of Canada. From its perspective, the successful mission in Iran, as well as Canada's condemnation of the Soviet Union's invasion of Afghanistan, indicated a shift in government policy. Under Joe Clark, the "leadership has sought deliberately to put Canada on a new course, staunchly in the Western camp and on the side of political humanism, after the long Trudeau regime that at times tended towards ambivalence," stated the paper.[63] Just as the *New York Times* had derided Diefenbaker's government as a "regime" in 1963, the *Journal*'s use of the same language illustrates the depth of disregard it held for Trudeau.

But the *Journal* had popped its own champagne bottle too soon. For who said Trudeau wouldn't be back?

REBOUND AND FINAL AU REVOIR

Trudeau had announced he would resign as Liberal leader, but the party convinced him to run once more in the 1980 election, as a new leader hadn't been chosen before Clark's government fell. On 18 February 1980, Trudeau, the man whom one American journalist had called "quixotic," brought his party back to power with a majority government. He vowed to quit after that term. Calling him a "born-again economic nationalist," Dusko Doder at the *Washington Post* reported that Trudeau was promising once again to expand Canadian control of the country's economy. [64] When it came to oil and gas, Doder said the prime minister's new goal was to have 50 percent of the industry under Canadian ownership by 1990. To achieve that, Trudeau introduced the National Energy Program (NEP), which favoured exploration by Canadian oil companies and Canadian buyouts of foreign subsidiaries.

The American press panned the new measure. At the business-minded *Wall Street Journal*, the NEP was called a "xenophobic" program and likened to a disease.[65] "Of course, Mr. Trudeau knows just what he's up to here," wrote the *Journal*. "He's trying to rally domestic support by pointing his finger at the big, bad giant to the north (ideologically) and south (geographically). It is sad to see Mr. Trudeau stricken with this malady."[66] In the *Washington Post*, the paper reported that the NEP had become an emotional sore point between Canada and the United States. Despite Canadian arguments that the program treated all foreign nations equally, the *Post* argued that with 57.6 percent of Canada's energy industry under American control, "it is not totally unreasonable to view this particular Trudeau effort as aimed principally at Americans."[67]

Media opinions aside, Trudeau's liberal and nationalistic policies were colliding with the conservative positions of the new Republican president on Pennsylvania Avenue. When Ronald Reagan warned Trudeau that he thought the NEP unfairly targeted American companies and Congress was upset, the prime minister snappily responded this had been part of his election mandate and Canadians strongly supported the program (which was not entirely true as many Western Canadians vehemently opposed it).[68] "On the Reagan stove, Canadian problems have been on the rearmost row of burners; and — to carry the analogy a bit further — Canada is about to boil over," wrote the *Chicago Tribune*.[69] Acid rain, energy, territorial fishing boundaries, the building of the Alaska gas pipeline — all were now sullying the cross-border relationship. "Enough is enough," declared the *Christian Science Monitor* in October 1981. "Despite genuine policy differences regarding a wide range of issues, the United States and Canada must take every step to stop the stream of insensitive words now coming from the two governments."[70]

That same month, the *Washington Post*, in an about-turn from earlier comments, urged Americans not to take the NEP as a personal slight. Despite the program, Canada remained more open to foreign ownership than did many other American allies. So it would be useful "for Americans to keep in mind that, for the Trudeau government, the central issue isn't oil or dollars, but a future constitution and national unity," counselled the paper.[71]

The *Post* was right. National unity had always been a top priority for Trudeau and now during his last term, the prime minister was doggedly and passionately pursuing a legacy of grandiose proportion — patriating the Constitution. On 17 April 1982, Queen Elizabeth II signed into law the Constitution Act, formally severing the last of the colonial ties that bound Canada to Britain.

But that achievement couldn't alleviate the economic downturn facing the country or the general negative attitudes toward Trudeau. In the early 1980s, Canada was hit by the worst recession in half a century and unemployment skyrocketed to nearly 13 percent. With Canada–U.S. relations also in disrepair, Trudeau rarely secured even objective press coverage in the United States. At the *Los Angeles Times*, Stanley Meisler wrote that the prime minister's arrogance and a fundamental flaw – an inability to communicate effectively with Canadians – were contributing to his downfall:

> Perhaps literature can explain Trudeau better than politics. He sometimes seems to resemble the Shakespearean tragic hero Coriolanus, whose pride as a leader made him unable and unwilling to win the favor of the people of Rome by flattering them. 'I would not buy their mercy at the price of one fair word,' he said. It was a statement that could have come from Trudeau.[72]

In 1983, the *Wall Street Journal* ran the headline "Pierre Trudeau's 15 Years of Failure."[73] The op-ed by Andy Stark, a Canadian studying at Harvard, positioned that the NEP and the Constitution were failures. Like Meisler at the *Los Angeles Times*, Stark drew upon history, quoting Voltaire's comment that "he who misunderstands his age, carries with him all the misfortunes of his age." Pierre Trudeau, Stark argued, "is a man of significant political misunderstanding, and he is not a man of his age – he was a generation out of date on the day he was elected. That, as Voltaire would say, has been the great misfortune of Canada, and to no small degree, of the world."[74]

On 29 February 1984, following his now-famous midnight walk during a snowstorm, Pierre Trudeau announced he would step down as Canada's prime minister. The news sparked a 16-point rally on the Toronto Stock Exchange in the composite share index and a 0.15-cent rise in the Canadian dollar as hope rose of a more pro-business successor as prime minister.[75]

The *Washington Post* and *Christian Science Monitor* wrote that Trudeau's greatest accomplishment after a political career spanning three decades and five American presidents was that Canada remained united despite regional differences and the threat from separatist movements in Quebec. From Toronto, the *Los Angeles Times'* Kenneth Freed bid farewell with these words: "Trudeau always seemed to know that he could not be accepted by his own people. 'A society which eulogizes the average citizen,' he said, 'is one which breeds mediocrity.' And if there is one thing nearly everyone agrees on here, it is that Trudeau was never mediocre."[76]

HELLO AGAIN USA!

With Pierre Trudeau taking his final pirouette, Canada was poised to enter a new political era; one that the American press hoped would prove beneficial for business and U.S.-Canada relations. John Turner, a former minister of justice and minister of finance during the early Trudeau years, re-entered the Liberal Party scene and was chosen as Trudeau's successor. Brian Mulroney led the opposition as leader of the Conservative Party. "Both Canadians conform more closely to the conventional American idea of a political leader," wrote Lansing Lamont in the *New York Times.* Lamont was former chief Canada correspondent for *Time* magazine and then-managing director for Canadian Affairs at the Americas Society. "If Mr. Trudeau's style blended flamboyance with cerebral hauteur, the new men are more predictable outgoing types: Mr. Turner, a cocky Kennedeyesque [sic] charmer, Mr. Mulroney, a Reganesque [sic] media performer with the most photogenic jaw since Jack Dempsey's."[77]

Just ten days after being sworn in as prime minister, Turner called an election for 4 September 1984. At the *Los Angeles Times,* an editorial pointed out that either Turner or Mulroney as prime minister would positively impact Canada and in turn, the United States. "Both are lawyers, both have close ties to business, both are committed to the importance of the private sector in helping Canada to economic recovery," the paper noted.[78]

Indeed, the future state of Canada's economy was of concern, especially to the business-minded *Wall Street Journal,* which wrote of Canada's "abysmal economic performance" as the United States successfully rebounded from a recession. The paper duly listed Canada's woes: gross national product (GNP) growth for 1985 was predicted to be flat or even negative, the unemployment rate still exceeded 11 percent, the federal budget deficit was projected to be around thirty billion dollars (Canadian) and the Canadian dollar hovered around 77 cents U.S. "In short, Canada should be cutting its burden of government, not increasing it," said the *Journal.* "But neither candidate appears to be offering Canadians that choice. The best they can hope for is that the party they choose will come up with the right answers after it is in power and has to struggle with economic problems that are not about to go away of their own accord." [79]

On Election Day, Canadians placed their economic fortunes in the Conservative Party, handing Tory candidates and their leader a sweeping victory with 211 of the 282 seats in the House of Commons. The Liberal Party, which had dominated the Canadian political scene for twenty-one years, was reduced to a humbling forty seats, its lowest ever. The *Chicago Tribune*'s Janet Cawley filed a story from Toronto, writing of Mulroney and his seemingly rapid ascent from lawyer and business executive to prime minister in little more than a year. "Sociable, witty and an instinctive politician, he has been called the 'greatest fondler and stroker of egos since Lyndon Baines Johnson plied the trade,'" she said. "But behind that charm is a steely resolve and a hard-edged pragmatism." [80]

With this overwhelming swing to the political right, the *New York Times* was confident testy bilateral relations would be soothed. Mulroney, after all, advocated for closer ties with the United States, more foreign investment, and increases in the defence budget. "Canada's relations with the United States are likely to be calmer now than they were in the last years under the volatile Mr. Trudeau," stated the paper. "[Mr. Mulroney] seems to understand that when the world's largest pair of trading partners diverge economically, it is Canada that tends to be the one that suffers." [81]

At the *Chicago Tribune*, the new prime minister was heartily acknowledged to be good not only for Canada, but also for the United States and NATO. Characterizing him as an "amiable free-trade conservative like his fellow Irishman, President Reagan," the paper editorialized that as Mulroney "has already demonstrated, the U.S. can expect a much more pragmatic and reasonable attitude on trade and energy matters and an end to the Yankee-baiting-for-its-own-sake practiced by Mr. Trudeau. Canada can now be expected to conduct its affairs in Washington not simply as an important neighbor but as a close friend." [82]

Mulroney was a conservative — that was clear. But lest Americans brush their brand of conservatism on Canada's political palette, Kenneth Freed at the *Los Angeles Times* had a few words of clarification. A conservative in Canada, he stressed, was not the same as one in the United States, the United Kingdom, or Western Europe. From strengthening social programs such as health care, unemployment insurance, and child care to tax reform that targeted wealthy Canadians, Freed said if Mulroney were running for office in the United States, his proposals would place him squarely in the centre or moderately left wing of the Democratic Party. So those, he wrote,

> ...who think a Conservative government in Ottawa means Canada will be joining the Reagan Administration and Great Britain's Prime Minister Margaret Thatcher in a "small c" conservative alliance to promote a free-market, entrepreneur-minded economic system with a hard-line anti-Soviet attitude will be disappointed. Those words, and that thinking, just don't mean the same thing in Canada.[83]

Although the style of conservatism may differ, Canada's move to the right boded well for American interests. By developing close friendships with Presidents Reagan and George H.W. Bush, Mulroney bound cross-border ties ever tighter, most prominently with the signing of the 1988 Free Trade Agreement, which was followed a few years later by the North American Free Trade Agreement (NAFTA). Ironically, this time it was the Conservatives who pushed free trade, a reversal of the roles played in 1911. Bilateral relations were strong; the American press spoke cordially of Canada.

But in politics, as in life, all good things eventually come to an end. And this time, there would be a nasty new tone in the Canada bashing.

★★★ CHAPTER 5 ★★★

HITTING BELOW THE BELT

2001 ONWARD

Canada is arguably the most deluded industrialized nation in the world. ~ *Jonah Goldberg, Editor,* National Review, *9 June 2006*

You can tell a lot about a nation's mediocrity index by learning that they invented synchronized swimming. Even more, by the fact that they're proud of it. ~ *Matt Labash, Senior writer,* The Weekly Standard, *21 March 2005*

The first years of the new millennium marked a turning point in how some American journalists and commentators viewed Canada. Bit by bit, story by story, exaggerated falsehoods – such as the September 11 terrorists snuck across the border from Canada – gained credibility as two principles of journalism – fairness and accuracy – were increasingly laid aside in favour of entertainment and cold cash. At the Canadian embassy in Washington, officials have spent years refuting the 9/11 untruth which pops up every so often in the hallowed halls of Congress and the controlled chaos of newsrooms. (The terrorists actually came from Saudi Arabia, the United Arab Emirates, Egypt, and Lebanon, and were trained in the United States – no Canadian links.)

Adding to the perpetuation of these blatant falsehoods were sinister and cynical undertones that largely didn't exist in earlier media coverage, even during the Champ Clark calls for annexation in 1911 or the Fenian runs on the fledgling Dominion in the late nineteenth century. Sure the *Los Angeles Times* may have compared Canada to that of a chippering chipmunk but the tone was dismissive; a scolding, superior "we are better" fashion. Canada also may have been portrayed as a backwater for simpletons, yet talk of annexation by Americans had implied the country held *some* value. They wouldn't have desired it otherwise. But now a question asked during the War of 1812 resurfaced. Could Canada be an enemy?

"You seem familiar, yet somehow strange—are you by any chance Canadian?"

This *New Yorker* cartoon aptly portrays American perception of Canadians by 2001 – similar yet mysteriously distinct. (*New Yorker*, 19 November 2001)

At first glance, that seems utterly absurd. Since the Canada–U.S. Free Trade Agreement came into effect on 1 January 1989, trade has tripled between the two countries. By 2006, almost two billion dollars in goods and services was crossing the border every day.[1] Canada is also a major player in supplying the United States with reliable energy. Since 1999, Canada has been the United States' largest supplier of oil, with statistics showing that in 2006 it provided more than 17 percent of U.S. crude and refined oil imports.[2] At more than two million barrels a day, that's a greater amount than any other country. Canada also supplies the U.S. with 86 percent of its natural gas imports, which represents 16 percent of American consumption.[3]

But the bare facts of economics, clothed as they are in the language of international trade, are far less titillating than witty exaggerations. Especially when fear casts a pall over an entire country.

STRIKES OF TERROR

The first details of 11 September 2001 are frozen in time in the initial stories reported by the media — the hijacking of four California-bound airplanes, the collapse of the World Trade Center's twin towers, a plane crashing into the Pentagon, another crash in a Pennsylvania field. Borders were closed, planes diverted, people evacuated. Thousands dead.

The Canadian government, now headed by Prime Minister Jean Chrétien, responded swiftly to the terrorist attacks in New York City and Washington, D.C. Within forty-five minutes, the country began accepting diverted aircraft. Two hundred twenty-four planes were ordered to land at airports across the country, leaving more than 33,000 passengers and crew stranded.[4] The stories of Canadian generosity in this crisis have been well-documented. In Gander, Newfoundland (population 10,000 souls), 12,000 people stepped off planes and were given food and shelter. "The effort here is staggering," wrote Kathy Borrus in the *Washington Post*. She had been on her way back to Washington after spending three weeks in Jordan on an USAID project. "From Gander to the surrounding towns of Norris Arm and Glenwood, our northern neighbors welcomed us."[5]

Marian Osher and her husband Chuck walked off their plane and found themselves in Halifax. In a letter to the *Washington Post*, Osher spoke of chefs preparing gourmet meals and buses bringing people to a shopping centre to buy underwear. "In a world beset with unspeakable, evil acts of terror, the Canadians provided us with an oasis of love," she wrote. "It is surprising that we never studied Canadian history in school, but now I want to learn more about our kind and caring northern neighbors."[6]

In the aftermath of the terrorist attacks, the outpouring of support and grief from Canadians received relatively scant attention in the American media and it seemed, even less by the American government. A short article in the *New York Times* highlighted a perceived snub that created an uproar in the Canadian press. "Canada Miffed at Bush Omission," read the headline, referring to President George W. Bush's speech to Congress in which he neglected to mention Canada when thanking nations for supporting the United States after the attacks. "When President Bush concluded his speech on Thursday night, a lot of Canadians were left feeling out in the cold," said the paper. "A few weeks ago, Mr. Bush made a point of calling Mexico America's oldest friend. That hurt, too."[7]

On the record, Canadian officials brushed off the omission. But neither they nor their counterparts on the other side of the border could know the extent to which unfolding events would strain American-Canadian relations.

In the media, a 24/7 news cycle had developed and in the immediate days following the 9/11 attacks, numerous reports sought to explain how the nineteen hijackers had been able to carry out their suicide missions. In those early hours, the finger of blame pointed north to Canada. Two days after the attacks, the *Washington Post*'s Dan Eggen reported, "Several of the hijackers may have entered the United States shortly before the attacks by taking a ferry from Nova Scotia to Portland, Maine, according to several sources."[8] The next day, a story by Eggen's colleagues DeNeen Brown and Ceci Connolly further detailed the suspected link between the terrorists and Canada. Under the headline "Suspects Entered Easily From Canada," the journalists reported the following:

Two suspects in Tuesday's terrorist attacks in the United States crossed the border from Canada with no known difficulty at a small, border entry in Coburn Gore, Maine, which is usually staffed by only one border inspection officer, a U.S. official said today. Another suspect appears to have slipped into the country from Canada at a border crossing at Jackman, Maine... while one or more may have ridden a ferry from Nova Scotia, docking at a port in Maine.[9]

Other media outlets publicized similar information. Among them, Barbara Crossette at the *New York Times* took a cautious approach, mentioning there had been reports of at least two terrorists entering the U.S. from Canada, but stressing the fact that both Paul Cellucci, U.S. Ambassador to Canada, and Canadian Foreign Minister John Manley said no connection had been confirmed. Still, Crossette noted that in recent years, "not only the United States but also several European countries, India and Sri Lanka have all been critical of what their officials see as a growing Canadian haven for a host of rebels and their fund-raisers."[10]

While a link between Canada and the 9/11 terrorists would never be found, the rumour would stubbornly persist. For some American journalists, previous information and events gave merit to storylines portraying Canada as a haven for terrorists. They pointed to criticism of the country's political asylum laws as lax and inadequate, with one frequently cited example being the case of "Millennium Bomber" Ahmed Ressam, an Algerian who was arrested in December 1999 as he crossed into Washington state with explosives to bomb Los Angeles International Airport on New Year's Eve. There were also several mentions in the *Washington Post* that the Canadian Security Intelligence Service (CSIS) had identified approximately 50 groups and 350 people as having ties to terrorism.[11]

With the United States seeking to close loopholes, attention soon focused on the Canada–U.S. border. Measuring a total of 8891 kilometres (5525 miles), Canada and the United States have often boasted of the International Boundary as the world's longest undefended border. From the American perspective, that distinction now proved problematic — how to keep the border open to trade while shutting it to terrorists. "The border is unusual — unusually undefended, unusually open, unusually busy and now under unusual scrutiny," an editorial in the *Los Angeles Times* stated concisely.[12] At the border, checkpoint delays were costing Canada too many fistfuls of dollars. Heightened security was hurting exports, leaving truckers at some border crossings idling for hours. The economies in border cities such as Niagara Falls and Windsor declined sharply, as carloads of American visitors simply seemed to vanish.

By mid-October, the media was reporting on the passage of anti-terrorism bills in Congress that included tripling the number of Border Patrol agents along the northern border. Around this time, John Manley announced that Canada would increase national security spending and tighten immigration laws. In December, the two countries would sign a "smart border" agreement that implemented travel controls and allowed pre-cleared goods to pass through customs quickly. "Chretien vowed to stand by President Bush 'every step of the way,'" concluded the above-mentioned *Los Angeles Times* editorial. "Chretien also vowed at home not to change Canada's character. Those goals aren't mutually exclusive. Even absent official proclamations, the harsher new realities of terror in North America... is likely to drive these two countries even closer together than anyone envisioned on Sept. 10."[280]

OFF TO WAR

Binational issues regarding trade and security dominated discussions in the wake of 9/11 — and so did pending military action in a new war against terrorism. With President Bush seeking allied support, the *New York Times*' Barbara Crossette wrote that in Ottawa, "Mr. Chretien is under intense political pressure, from both right and left, as he faces decisions on what to promise Washington."[14] On the right, Crossette noted, were demands by conservatives for a firm commitment of military troops and a clampdown on domestic asylum laws; on the left, including many within the Liberal Party, were calls for Canada to refrain from automatically heading off with the United States on a warpath.

Whatever the debate in Canada, the American media wasn't overly interested other than to mention during the first days of air strikes on Afghanistan in early October 2001 that Canada had committed to assisting future operations with military aircraft, ships, and approximately two thousand troops. From Toronto, the *Washington Post*'s DeNeen Brown said any sense of security Canadians might have felt evaporated as al-Qaida warned that nations siding with the United States would be marked enemies. "Canada is not accustomed to being considered an enemy in the world, much less a potential terrorist target," she wrote. "The Maple Leaf attached to a suitcase has long symbolized peace."[15] But peace was now perceived as elusive. An Ipsos-Reid poll revealed that 66 percent of those surveyed feared there could be a terrorist attack in Canada.[16] Despite that concern, the same poll indicated more than 70 percent of Canadians supported the "War on Terrorism" in Afghanistan.

That approval rating would plummet in the coming years and become a divisive issue in Canadian politics. A black mark for many occurred 18 April 2002, six months into the war, when four Canadian soldiers were killed and eight others injured after an American F-16 pilot dropped a laser-guided 225-kilogram (500-pound) bomb on a live-fire night exercise near Kandahar. Canada was in mourning. In a letter sent to the *Washington Post*, Robert Stasko in Toronto told readers he was perplexed. "What puzzles me is the limited coverage of this disaster in the U.S. media," he wrote. "Had Canadian troops killed U.S. soldiers via 'friendly fire,' there would be hell to pay. Instead, the arrest of Hollywood actor Robert Blake hogs the headlines."[17]

As if in response to Stasko's musings, an editorial in the *Los Angeles Times* a few days later said that while sad, tragic happenings were a fact of war. "The overheated reaction of some Canadians highlights a perennial delicacy in U.S.–Canadian relations, even without Canadians serving under U.S. command," it stated. "As the physically larger and less populated half of North America, Canada has long displayed a penchant for perceiving slights and feeling underappreciated, even abused."[18] Still, the editorial warned that American interests would be better served if the government were more sensitive to foreign cultures, including Canada's. It noted that although President Bush had spoken to Prime Minister Chrétien after the bombing, he had been slow to offer public condolences. Nearly a year later, *New York Times* correspondent Clifford Krauss filed a story from Hubbards, Nova Scotia, the hometown of Pte. Richard Green, one of the soldiers killed in the friendly fire incident. "In Canada, a nation often obsessed with its next-door superpower, the deaths of the four soldiers have come to epitomize the widely held perception that the United States takes Canada for granted," he wrote. "The incident has also become an enduring symbol of the sacrifice that Canadians believe they make when the United States is in need but that is not reciprocated on issues critical to Canada."[19] It was now early 2003 and the United States was justifying its case for war in Iraq. Added to that heated discussion, a flurry of crises would beset Canada. It would be a watershed year in Canada–U.S. relations — and insults would be hurled from both sides of the border.

NO LONGER NICE

The mudslinging actually began in late 2002. While Prime Minister Jean Chrétien had enjoyed a good working relationship with his golf buddy President Bill Clinton, there was a gaping divide between the ideological stances of President George Bush, the Texan cowboy, and Chrétien, the French-Canadian lawyer. Whether deliberate or unintentional, the list of perceived slights kept getting longer. Critics pointed at Bush's decision to make his first trip as president to Mexico instead of Canada, along with his failure to thank Canada during the post-9/11 speech to Congress and his delay in issuing public condolences following the friendly fire incident in Afghanistan. Now, as the Bush administration scrambled to amass allied support for an invasion of Iraq, Canada held back. Chrétien challenged the president to show proof that Saddam Hussein had weapons of mass destruction and the intent to use them.[20] That position — as well as Canada's response to anti-terrorism measures in the United States — propelled America's increasingly influential conservative media to whip out its verbal assault arsenal.

On 31 October 2002, political commentator and former Republican presidential hopeful Pat Buchanan labelled

Canada a "Soviet Canuckistan" on his MSNBC show *Buchanan and Press*.[21] He was apparently striking back at Canadian criticism of post-9/11 security rules that required fingerprinting and registering Arab Canadians seeking to enter the United States.

Jonah Goldberg, editor-at-large of the conservative *National Review Online*, had a few choice words to say too. With political pundits and military strategists examining the merits of an attack on Iraq, Goldberg proposed action of a different sort — bomb Canada. In November 2002, the *National Review*'s magazine cover featured Royal Canadian Mounted Police officers astride their horses with the word "Wimps!" stamped across the page in bold letters. The conversation-inducing image was accompanied by Goldberg's equally provocative article "Bomb Canada: The Case for War."

Granted, Goldberg wasn't calling for a full-scale attack on America's northern neighbour. Such a conquest was unnecessary, he said because "all Canada needs is to be slapped around a little bit, to be treated like a whining kid who's got to start acting like a man."[22] The problem, Goldberg wrote, was that Canada just didn't cut it anymore when it came to military strength. Prime Minister Jean Chrétien's hesitancy to contribute troops for an Iraq invasion was a moot point. Even if the country did, "Canada's role would be like Jamaica's at the Winter Olympics — a noble and heartwarming gesture, but a gesture nonetheless," Goldberg quipped. "Despite Canada's self-delusions, it is, quite simply, not a serious country anymore. It is a northern Puerto Rico with an EU sensibility."[23] Ouch.

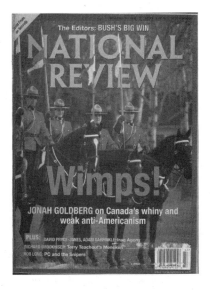

As Canada debated whether to join in an invasion of Iraq, Jonah Goldberg at the *National Review* offered a provocative alternative – bomb Canada. (*National Review*, 25 November 2002)

To snap Canada out of its reliance on U.S. military might, Goldberg suggested the following:

> We certainly don't need the burden of turning "the world's longest undefended border" into one of the world's longest defended ones. And that's why a little invasion is precisely what Canada needs.... If the U.S. were to launch a quick raid into Canada, blow up some symbolic but unoccupied structure — Toronto's CN Tower, or perhaps an empty hockey stadium — Canada would rearm overnight.
>
> Indeed, Canada might even be forced to rethink many of its absurd socialist policies in order to pay for the costs involved in protecting itself from the Yankee peril. Canada's neurotic anti-Americanism would be transformed into manly resolve. The U.S. could quickly pretend to be frightened that it had messed with the wrong country, and negotiate a fragile peace with the newly ornery Canadians. In a sense, the U.S. owes it to Canada to slap it out of its shame-spiral. That's what big brothers do.[24]

If models of family dynamics are to be brought into this discussion, then it's relevant to point out that while older siblings may be bullies, younger ones can be whiny name callers. There were certainly some incidents of that during this phase of the Canadian–American relationship. Around the time Jonah Goldberg's article was heading to the printing press, Françoise Ducros, Chrétien's director of communications, referred to President Bush as a "moron" during a conversation with a journalist at the NATO summit in Prague.[25] The prime minister initially refused her letter of resignation, but accepted it a week later under pressure from opposition parties.

Liberal member of Parliament Carolyn Parrish put another public face to the groundswell of anti-Americanism. With war in Iraq imminent, Parrish, in a moment of true television serendipity, was caught on camera saying, "Damn Americans. I hate those bastards" as she walked away from a scrum (an impromptu news conference).[26] The Washington Post's "In The Loop" columnist Al Kamen wrote, "So this was her 'personal opinion' of President Bush? Or maybe it wasn't her opinion at all and someone channeled into her brain? This keeps happening and Americans will think the Canadians really don't like us and think we're either stupid or bastards — or both. Hmmm... You know, that timber tariff is a piddling 27 percent. Surely that could be ratcheted up."[27]

Parrish apologized to Parliament and U.S. Ambassador Paul Cellucci, but more than a year and a half later in November 2004, she followed up her comments by stomping on a President Bush doll for a taping of the CBC satirical comedy show, *This Hour Has 22 Minutes*.[28] By then, Paul Martin had become prime minister, and he finally expelled her from the Liberal caucus.

In the weeks leading up to the invasion of Iraq, Canada sought to settle intense international debate on the validity of such an attack through the diplomatic channels of the United Nations. The world, Prime Minister Jean Chrétien said, "must speak and act through the UN Security Council."[29] At the *New York Times*, Nicholas Kristof, dryly commenting on the recent spate of anti-American comments in Canada, observed that America's international reputation must be truly suffering indeed. "When even the Canadians, normally drearily polite, get colorfully steamed at us, we know the rest of the world is apopleptic [sic]," he wrote. "Canada's incivility is a reminder that the U.S. and its allies are slugging one another to death while Iraq watches from the sidelines."[30] Of course, Kristof added, some Americans would argue it didn't matter that the United States was being perceived as an aggressor or as he called it, "the world's newest Libya. If the Canadians don't like us, we can always exercise the military option and push our border up to 54 – 40"[31] — a direct reference to the Oregon boundary dispute in the early nineteenth century when the United States and Britain were negotiating possession of the Pacific Northwest (from today's Alaska-British Columbia border down to the Oregon-California border). Tongue-in-cheek remarks aside, Kristof's concern was real; global attitudes did matter, especially those of allies.

On 20 March 2003, the United States and its "coalition of the willing" invaded Iraq. Canada was not among them. In fact, Canadians were behaving, well, very *un-Canadian*. Fans booed loudly as "The Star-Spangled Banner" was sung at hockey games. Others burned the American flag.[32] The *Washington Post* reported that Prime Minister Chrétien had to ask his cabinet members and the public to stop making anti-American comments.[33] To counter this negativity, some Canadians organized pro-America rallies.

But it didn't take long before practical considerations overrode emotional objections. At the *Chicago Tribune*, Dan Mihalopoulos wrote that just weeks into the military campaign, "some Canadians are becoming worried that their anti-war stance could engender scorn and economic punishment from the United States, Canada's top foreign investor and partner in the North American Free Trade Agreement."[34] Canada's corporate community was so concerned about losing business that Mihalopoulos reported a delegation of approximately a hundred business leaders was heading to Washington, D.C. He also mentioned that, noticing a shift in public opinion, Chrétien's government was supporting a motion stating Canada's "'hope that the U.S.-led coalition accomplishes its mission as quickly as possible.'"[35]

THE SCHISM WIDENS

If conflicting stances on Iraq had placed a chill on cross-border relations, then further unpredicted events would make them positively frosty. *New York Times* correspondent Clifford Krauss wrote of 2003 as a year remembered in "biblical terms, as a year of plagues."[36] Krauss was actually reflecting on how events had affected Canada's tourism industry, but his words aptly describe the situation in which the country found itself. Along with the political divides over Iraq, Canada dealt with an outbreak of SARS (severe acute respiratory syndrome) in March. The illness would kill forty-four people in Toronto. Then on 20 May, lab results confirmed that a cow in Alberta had bovine spongiform encephalopathy (BSE) or mad cow disease. The BSE case prompted the American government to ban all imports of Canadian beef immediately, a decision that sent the country's beef industry into a death spiral, with an estimated loss of eleven million dollars a day.[37] A two-decades-old trade dispute over Canadian softwood lumber would also fester, with American interests competing against Canadian ones. There were raging wildfires in British Columbia and a massive power outage that affected Ontario and the northeastern United States. In the *Chicago Tribune*, Kevin Christiano, a sociology professor at the University of Notre Dame, summed it up this way:

> In a kind of cosmic convergence of truly wretched publicity, news stories come beaming south about our northern cousins that seem practically designed to anger, annoy or scare Americans. The piqued politicians, reluctance on Iraq, laxity of laws, the spread of deadly diseases among animals and humans: Each is part of a string of events that threaten to upset Americans' notions of Canada as a safe, sane and supportive neighbor.[38]

At the *New York Times*, Clifford Krauss wasn't interested so much in disagreements over trade and safety; those tended to flare up periodically. But Prime Minister Jean Chrétien's Liberal government was pushing a social agenda that made many Americans cringe. There was official endorsement regarding the legalization of same-sex marriage and a proposal decriminalizing small amounts of marijuana. Krauss reported that these types of policies reflected a shift in social and cultural values, as opposed to political ones. It seemed, he wrote, that "from gay marriage to drug use to church attendance, a chasm has opened up on social issues that go to the heart of fundamental values. A more distinctive Canadian identity — one far more in line with European sensibilities — is emerging and generating new frictions with the United States."[39]

In the American media, some journalists didn't bother hiding their disappointment at Canada's left swing on social policies and its anti-war position on Iraq. Commenting on what he described as the new "Berkeley North," David Montgomery at the *Washington Post* bemoaned the passing of the stereotypes Americans had held for so long:

What happened to that clean cold land of Mounties, Dudley Do-Right, loons on lakes, loons on coins, cheese on french fries? What of the goofy, front-teeth-missing, bad-haircut, lovable beer-and-doughnut civilization of hosers like Bob and Doug McKenzie, the characters created by Canadian comedians Rick Moranis and Dave Thomas? Eh? Bob would ponder conundrums like: "What is a six-pack equal to in metric conversion?" That's a Canada we recognize, where everyone speaks in a crisp nasal deadpan, even the French. It is the home of a self-deprecating and polite-to-the-point-of-invisible people.[40]

When it came to casting a typical image of Canadians, conservative magazine the *Weekly Standard* had some of its own. Reporting from Vancouver with an article headlined "Welcome to Canada: The Great White Waste of Time," Matt Labash opined that Canadians were "a docile, Zamboni-driving people who subsist on seal casserole and Molson."[41] These northern neighbours, he wrote, "are bizarrely obsessed with us, binge-eating out of our cultural trough, then pretending it tastes bad. Plainly the two things Canada needs most are a mirror and a good psychiatrist."[42] Labash's thoughts about Canada as a whole were no less effusive. In his view, the country was an "idyllic Rainbowland," "the perfect place for American quitters," and akin to a mildewy attic where you could stash "Nazi war criminals, drawing-room socialists, and hockey goons."

Meanwhile, Fox News anchor John Gibson aired his thoughts directly to Canadians in an article that appeared in *Maclean's* magazine, wishing Canada an un-happy birthday on 1 July 2005. "If things are so good in the multicultural, egalitarian quasi-socialist Canada," he wisecracked, "why do so many leave to come to the fearsome jungles of America? Was there a potato famine up north that we missed?"[43]

If some in the American press were reverting to the type of mockery that had been popular around the turn of the last century, conservative television commentators went one step further, repeatedly taking verbal aim at Canada with exaggerations and blatant lies.

DOWNWARD SPIRAL

If one wants to hear controversial statements, a good place to listen in is cable news, for there, imbedded in the hard news updates on crime, politics, and world events are programs distinctly shaped around engaging and outspoken personalities. Think of CNN's Nancy Grace and Fox's Bill O'Reilly. The idea behind these shows is not hard-core news analysis per se, but often a form of discussion that entertains as much as it — or perhaps even more — than it informs.

In late 2004, President Bush made his first official state visit to Canada. The president had previously cancelled a scheduled trip in 2003, saying he needed to stay in Washington because of the war in Iraq. The announcement had led to speculation that the United States was giving Canada and Prime Minister Jean Chrétien the diplomatic cold shoulder for not sending troops to aid in the war effort there. Now, with a change in Liberal leadership and Paul Martin as prime minister, Bush headed to Canada for two days.

His public welcome party reflected the cold temperatures. As Bush arrived in Ottawa on 30 November, an estimated five thousand protesters gathered, shouting "Go Home" and other slogans as they lined the motorcade route and marched on Parliament Hill.[44] Similar rallies took place in cities across the country. CNN's conservative bow-tied host and commentator Tucker Carlson had some retorts of his own. "Without the U.S., Canada is essentially Honduras, but colder and much less interesting.... Canada needs the United States. The United States does not need Canada," he argued while interviewing Carolyn Parrish on *Wolf Blitzer Reports*.[45] That same day, while co-hosting CNN's *Crossfire* and talking about the protests with Canadian talk show host Ken Rockburn, Carlson declared, "Canada's essentially — essentially a made-in-Taiwan version of the United States."[46] Over at Fox News, conservative political pundit Ann Coulter was taking part in a panel discussion on *Hannity & Colmes*, and had this to say about her northern neighbour:

> COULTER: Conservatives, as a general matter, take the position that you should not punish your friends and reward your enemies. And Canada has become trouble recently.

It's I suppose it's always, I might add, the worst Americans who end up going there. The Tories after the Revolutionary War, the Vietnam draft dodgers after Vietnam. And now after this election, you have the blue-state people moving up there. [...]

COULTER: There is also something called, when you're allowed to exist on the same continent of the United States of America, protecting you with a nuclear shield around you, you're polite and you support us when we've been attacked on our own soil. They [Canada] violated that protocol. [...]

COULTER: They better hope the United States doesn't roll over one night and crush them. They are lucky we allow them to exist on the same continent. [...]

COULTER: We could have taken them [Canada] over so easily.

ALAN COLMES: We could have taken them over? Is that what you want?

COULTER: Yes, but no. All I want is the western portion, the ski areas, the cowboys, and the right-wingers. [...]

COULTER: They don't even need to have an army, because they are protected, because they're on the same continent with the United States of America. If we were not the United States of America, Canada I mean, we're their trading partner. We keep their economy afloat. [...]

ELLIS HENICAN [Newsday columnist]: We share a lot of culture and a lot of interests. Why do we want to have to ridicule them and be deeply offended if they disagree with us?

COULTER: Because they speak French.

COLMES: There's something else I want to point out about the French. Is it's fashionable again on your side to denounce the French.

COULTER: We like the English-speaking Canadians.[47]

A few months later, the *New York Times'* Clifford Krauss reported in a much more staid fashion that as President Bush prepared to greet Prime Minister Martin and President Vicente Fox of Mexico at his ranch in Crawford, Texas, things could be tense as differences over trade and the United States' missile defence system added to previous strains over Iraq. But then, he argued, that wasn't anything new. "With the possible exception of France, no traditional ally has been more consistently at odds with the United States than has Canada," Krauss wrote. [48] He then listed past bilateral grievances from the Cuban missile crisis to Cuban trade, Vietnam War draft dodgers and the Kyoto Protocol. "While the leaders always claim the greatest fondness for one another, more often than not they have not gotten along very well," he said. "When they have, Canadian leaders have sometimes had to pay a political price."[49]

As if to emphasize that point, another potent spate of Canada-bashing remarks was unleashed in December 2005 as a heated election campaign pitting Prime Minister Martin against Conservative Party leader Stephen Harper got underway. On 7 December, during a United Nations climate change conference in Montreal, Martin chastised the United States, calling it a "reticent nation" when it came to global environmental policies. U.S. Ambassador to Canada David Wilkins warned Martin to tone down the rhetoric or risk damaging cross-border relations. "It may be smart election-year politics to thump your chest and criticize your friend and your number one trading partner constantly," Wilkins said during a speech to the Canadian Club in Ottawa. "But it is a slippery slope, and all of us should hope that it doesn't have a long-term impact on the relationship."[50] This of course, provided Martin with the opportunity to use the time-honoured "anti-American" election shtick and he retorted that as prime minister, he was the one who could stand up to the United States and defend Canada. From his television studio, Tucker Carlson gleefully entered the verbal fray with two comments in particular that would rile up the Canadian press.

Here's the problem with telling Canada to stop criticizing the United States: It only eggs them on. Canada is essentially a stalker, stalking the United States, right? Canada has little pictures of us in its bedroom, right? Canada spends all of its time thinking about the United States, obsessing over the United States. It's unrequited love between Canada and the United States. We, meanwhile, don't even know Canada's name. We pay no attention at all.[51]

Canada is a sweet country. It is like your retarded cousin you see at Thanksgiving and sort of pat him on the head. You know, he's nice, but you don't take him seriously.[52]

Tucker Carlson's colourful and non-politically correct jabs would seem outlandish to anyone who has even the simplest knowledge of Canada–U.S. relations. Of course, the United States pays attention to Canada; it also relies heavily on Canadian imports. These types of remarks can be easily dismissed with most observers saying they would have no long-term effect on American public opinion of Canada.

But following Martin's statements at the UN climate change conference, there was a darker side to some of the remarks lobbed from the American side of the border, with some not-so-subtle hints questioning Canada's allegiance to the United States. Fox News host Neil Cavuto asked on his show *Your World*, "[C]ould our neighbors to the north soon be our enemies?"[53]

Criticism of Canada intensified after the invasion of Iraq in 2003, with some conservative commentators, including Fox News host Neil Cavuto, questioning Canada's loyalty. (Fox News, 14 December 2005)

The United States was losing patience with Canada after all the criticism over Iraq and "well, pretty much everything else," he announced. Were Canadians getting too big for their britches, Cavuto speculated as an on-screen text read "Canada: An Enemy of the United States of America?"[54]

Two days later, an op-ed piece in the *Washington Times* — a competitor of the *Washington Post* in the nation's capital — raised the same question.

Douglas MacKinnon, one-time White House and Pentagon official, and press secretary to former Senator Bob Dole, asked, "Can Canada really be considered our 'friend' anymore?"[55] Taking a swipe at his family's former homeland, MacKinnon said the question had to be raised because "the Canadian government not only willingly allows Islamic terrorists into their country, but does nothing to stop them from entering our nation."[56] It seemed to escape MacKinnon's notice that entering the United States required passing through *American* customs checkpoints, not Canadian ones.

At Fox News, there was also talk of Canada harbouring terrorists. During a conversation with Bill O'Reilly on *The O'Reilly Factor* in 2004, Fox anchor John Gibson said, "Canada's a joke. I mean, they're rife with terrorists, they can't find them up there."[57] O'Reilly later picked up the mantra in 2006, saying on his radio program, *The Radio Factor with Bill O'Reilly,* that "They've got all kinds of Muslim crazies up in Canada running around."[58]

Even the *New Yorker* magazine contributed to the Canada bashing, albeit in a less direct fashion. Trailing the spate of harsh anti-Canadian comments, in a 2008 article on — of all things — the peril of the penny as a unit of currency, writer David Owen alluded to lingering frustrations with Canada. This despite the country's swing to the right with the election of Conservative Party leader Stephen Harper as prime minister in February 2006, the resolution of trade grievances on softwood lumber and BSE, and widespread American disapproval of the war in Iraq. Quoting a Canadian study suggesting the government not follow American currency policy because the U.S.'s conservative nature and love of symbolism had resisted moves to adopt the metric system and abolish the dollar bill for a coin, Owen wrote "This sort of slur from an (alleged) ally probably isn't worth going to war over, especially now that its money is sometimes worth more than ours."[59] Perhaps this was Owen's flaccid attempt at crafting a joke, but the use of "alleged" seemed to imply that either a) questioning Canada's loyalty was now "common sense," b) he was slyly planting seeds of doubt about Canada in his readers' minds, or c) Owen was the *New Yorker*'s version of Jonah Goldberg — less abrasive, more eloquent, but equally a pain in the royal Canadian butt.

Still, the larger question looms: Why had Canada once again become the favourite stomping doll for some American journalists and commentators? And what did it all mean?

Compare the sheer number of words thrown about during a daily news cycle and it's apparent that the amount of anti-Canadianism in the American media is miniscule. So then, a comment here, another one there, what could be the harm? It's not that simple. Take for example, the negative press and calls for french fries to be renamed "freedom fries" in 2002 after France expressed strong opposition to the American push for a United Nations mandate authorizing military action against Iraq. Charting American opinion of France, Gallup polls show that from 1992 until 2002, between 70 and 79 percent of Americans held a favourable view of the country.[1] But within the span of one year, those friendly feelings plummeted to 34 percent. By 2008, despite five years of steady increases, the percentage of Americans with a positive view of the French still hadn't reached pre-2002 levels.

What's even more interesting is that as this favourability rating deteriorated between 2002 and 2003, so did trade relations. A study published by the Centre for Economic Performance at the London School of Economics and Political Science found that American imports from France dropped roughly 15 percent while U.S. exports there decreased by approximately 8 percent when compared to other OECD or Eurozone nations.[2] The study also reported a similar drop in American business and vacation trips to France.

Analysis of American feelings towards Canada from 1992 until 2008 reveals a similar, although not nearly as drastic statistical tumble in fuzzy feelings during the first years of the war in Iraq. From 1992 to 2002, Gallup polls document a steady favourability rating hovering between 89 and 92 percent.[3] But beginning in 2003, Gallup charts a slight drop in positive opinions of Canada, bottoming out at 86 percent in 2005 before climbing back up to 92 percent in 2008.

What's interesting is that Gallup's recorded dip in favourability ratings differs widely from similar surveys conducted by the Pew Research Center for the People and the Press. Asking a nearly identical question —"Please tell me if you have a very favorable, somewhat favorable, somewhat unfavorable or very unfavorable opinion of Canada"— the Pew Global Attitudes Project found that in the summer of 2002, 83 percent of Americans held a favourable impression of Canada, but less than a year later, in May 2003, that opinion had declined to 65 percent.[4] By 2005, while the favourability rating had jumped to 76 percent, it was still below the poll results of 2002.

Explanations of this discrepancy vary, but it's worth noting that the Pew Global Attitudes Project records a much higher number of "Don't know/Refused" responses — 11 to 14 percent compared to Gallup's "No opinion" rates of 2 to 4 percent. And although the polls were taken during the same period, from 2003 to 2005 there were several abrupt differences between the two countries on various political, economic, and social issues which could have negatively impacted American opinions depending on the month in which a survey was conducted. Regardless, the overall trend in American attitudes towards Canada reveals two key findings. First, unlike what happened with France, cross-border trade remained strong even when American popular opinion of Canada became less favourable. Second, it seems that the war in Iraq negatively affected attitudes towards Canada more than the erroneously reported Canadian link to the 9/11 terrorists. Perhaps this is due to the abundance of positive media coverage detailing how Canada helped the United States during and after the 9/11 attacks. In their own way, these reports may have balanced out the negative terrorist stories. But once the afterglow faded, it seems American public opinion fell as the media took aim at Canada during the build up to and start of the war in Iraq.

Chronicling attitudes from the Canadian side of the border, surveys by the Pew Research Center reveal that sentiments were only slightly more positive than those in the United States, with America's image in Canada falling from a 72 percent favourability rating in 2002 to 63 percent by 2003, a nine-point decline.[5] But the report also noted an intriguing difference in the Canadian psyche. While Canadians' view of the United States as a country dipped, their opinion of the American people did not.

A 2006 report by The Strategic Counsel in Toronto reported a parallel schizophrenic tendency in Canadians over a slightly longer time frame.

The study showed that in 2001, 23 percent of Canadians considered Canada's relationship with the United States to be at "the best of friends" level (Table 5.1). By March 2006 that had dropped to 11 percent.[6] Yet the same poll revealed that 70 percent of Canadians said they respected Americans while fundamentally disagreeing with the U.S. government (Table 5.2).[7]

TABLE 5.1 How do Canadians see our relationship with the United States?

	Nov 2001	Nov 2002	Nov 2003	Mar 2006
Like family to each other	10%	5%	4%	6%
The best of friends	23%	17%	10%	11%
Friends, but not especially close	47%	49%	45%	46%
Cordial, but distant with each other	18%	25%	32%	30%

Source: The Strategic Counsel, *Canadians' Perceptions and Attitudes Towards the United States.* 27 March 2006.

It appeared Canadians were mentally separating their personal opinion of Americans formed during holidays, business trips, and everyday encounters from dissatisfaction with the Bush administration's policies, which included two wars. Still, friendly perceptions were slow to rebound, with The Strategic Counsel finding that between 2006 and 2008 the percentage of Canadians who considered Canada's relations with the U.S. at a "best friends" level increased by a mere two percentage points to 13 percent, considerably below the 23 percent reported in the wake of the 9/11 terrorist attacks.[8] This dismal rise in favourability ratings seems to suggest deeper issues than policy differences that shift with the changing of administrations, for by the time

TABLE 5.2 Level of agreement with the following statement: "I value and respect the United States and its citizens — it's just that I disagree fundamentally with their government."

	Mar 2006
NET Agree	**70%**
Very much agree	29%
Somewhat agree	41%
Somewhat disagree	17%
Very much disagree	9%
NET Disagree	**26%**

Source: The Strategic Counsel, *Canadians' Perceptions and Attitudes Towards the United States.* 27 March 2006.

the 2006 and 2008 polls were conducted, the bilateral relationship was once again viewed in positive terms by both governments. Possible reasons for this gap between diplomatic sentiment and popular public opinion abound. Although officially committed to efforts in Afghanistan, Canadians were becoming increasingly weary as the number of war casualties climbed. There was also the divergence in cultural and social values, as well as the fact that many of this decade's twenty-something Canadians grew up under the shadow of 9/11 and their college minds were shaped during one of the most tumultuous periods in Canada–U.S. relations.

Whatever the cause, personal opinions are shaped by circumstances, experiences, relationships — and even persuasive arguments voiced by the media. That's what makes the repeated negativity towards Canada on Fox News troubling as the network influences millions of Americans. Launched in 1996, Fox News Channel quickly became the fastest growing cable network in the United States. In 2005, for instance, the prime-time audience for Fox News increased by 9 percent while its main cable rivals experienced declines — 11 percent at CNN and 2 percent at MSNBC.[9] That success tapered off in 2006 when, for the first time, Fox News experienced a double-digit drop in viewership.[10] Still, the Republican-leaning network has continued to secure the largest number of viewers, with its programs dominating the Top 10 list of cable news shows.[11] Bill O'Reilly's *The O'Reilly Factor* alone has averaged a nightly audience of roughly two million, making it the most-watched show on the cable news networks.[12] So when O'Reilly or other conservative Fox News hosts and commentators have taken a swing at Canada, plenty of Americans have noticed.

Of particular concern are the remarks about Canada as a haven for terrorists. Unlike clearly outrageous comments that have been made — such as Tucker Carlson comparing Canada to Honduras — these ones have struck a menacing note that pry on new-found fears. In the aftermath of the 9/11 attacks, Americans were inundated with colour-coded terrorist threat barometers and media updates on Guantanamo Bay detainees. In this tensely suspicious environment, when public figures like Bill O'Reilly have insinuated that Canada harbours terrorists, or members of Congress including then-Senator Hillary Rodham Clinton as well as Homeland Security Secretary Janet Napolitano have mentioned that the 9/11 terrorists crossed into the United States from Canada, it lends automatic validity to baseless rumours undermining Canadian security and the country's image.[13] Even if retractions are issued after a comment was made — as in the case of Democratic Representative Rubén Hinojosa of Texas who told a congressional committee "as we all know, terrorists entered the U.S. from Canada on Sept. 11, 2001"[14] — there's no way of knowing whether the people who read or listened to the original statement also heard the apology.

The grossly exaggerated and often false statements about Canada also reflect the realities of today's media landscape, especially that of television. In a throwback to the days of William Randolph Hearst, Joseph Pulitzer, and yellow journalism, the push for higher ratings and larger corporate profits in the United States has encouraged a paler but still potent kind of sensationalism. Take for instance the headline-grabbing coverage of socialite Paris Hilton's stint in a Los Angeles county jail for a probation violation in 2007.

The gnarled roots of this kind of celebrity-saturated, quick-flash news creep back to the 1970s and the proliferation of news consulting firms. One such company, Frank N. Magid Associates, has been hugely influential although little known to the public. Derided by some journalists for its effect on local television news, Magid pioneered the use of market research and consultancy work to revamp newscasts into the "action news" style that is seen today.[15] There's the flashy graphics and car chases; short hyped-up stories; chatter between anchors and reporters; and an extraordinary focus on clothes and appearance, which has led to impeccably coiffed and dressed staff who look like they've stepped out of a fashion magazine — and never walked outside of the newsroom. While the strategies hawked by news consultants like Magid have raised station ratings and profits, it has cost journalism dearly. For what else can be expected when a newsroom's premise is based on giving the audience what they want to see instead of what they should know?

The resulting shallowness worries those in the profession. In the 2008 *State of the News Media* report, almost 80 percent of journalists surveyed thought the news didn't pay enough attention to complex issues; more than 60 percent said the line between reporting and commentary was becoming increasingly blurred.[16]

This is where commentators like Bill O'Reilly come in. With the Internet providing instant access to the latest stories, and around-the-clock news coverage hampering the popularity and profits of newspapers and traditional television evening newscasts, cable news networks are in a tooth and nail fight for viewership. In competing for the attention of Americans, the cable outlets are using cutting-edge graphics (CNN's touch-screen election maps), controversial headlines (remember Fox's "Canada: Friend or Foe?"), and punchy slogans (Fox's "We Report. You Decide."). This intense rivalry for the eyes and ears of the public has lent pseudo-legitimacy to rash generalizations and exaggerations. So O'Reilly is allowed to say Canada is a terrorist haven because the controversial statement might bring in a larger audience, which means a bump in ratings, greater profits, and so on up the corporate ladder of monetary success. In this kind of system, commentators are rewarded for their inaccuracies, fear mongering, and top-down approach.

There's another side to the proliferation of cable news networks and news blogs: they encourage people to turn to sources that reflect their own views. Gone are the days when Walter Cronkite's CBS evening newscasts gathered Americans of differing political stripes around the same television set. News has become much more partisan with "conservatives" turning to Fox News and *National Review Online* while "liberals" stick to CNN and the *Huffington Post*. A classic example is blogger Chris Kelly's (no, not the Ottawa Senators hockey player) entry on the *Huffington Post* when the *National Review*'s cruise ship stopped in Vancouver in August 2007. Referring back to Jonah Goldberg's "Bomb Canada" article in 2002, Kelly wrote, "I hope no one in Canada gets offended when people like Jonah Goldberg write ugly nonsense. They don't really mean it. They're just trying to be vile, as a substitute for how men might talk."[17] Before criticizing Goldberg, Kelly took aim at the publication itself, saying the "*National Review* isn't really a magazine at all, it's just a club where a certain kind of chin-challenged endomorph can sniff deeply of his own fingers and experiment with cruelty as a counterintuitive answer to everything."[18] This polarization of the media into two camps, one championing liberalism and the other conservatism, has led to an "us against them" mentality that's increasingly reflected in conversations among Americans (imagine the horror among my Democratic friends if they knew I chatted with Republicans and vice versa – I say this only partly in jest).

The partisan lines that have been etched so firmly into the American landscape reveal the United States is in the midst of an identity crisis, one that places average Americans at a crossroads when it comes to their country's future direction. The question they're faced with is this: Will the United States remain standing on the foundation of its conservative, capitalist past or will it embrace the values of social liberalism espoused by Canada and Western Europe? The 2008 election further underscored this stark choice. Obama, who evoked memories of Pierre Trudeau's first campaign with his Obamakins and inspirational calls for change, campaigned on platforms of universal health care, tuition tax breaks, and expansion of the Family and Medical Leave Act – policies that all sound very Canadian-like. On the Republican side, Senator John McCain stumped market-based solutions to fix the country's economic, health, and education woes, and went so far as to declare that Obama's policies sounded "a lot like socialism."[19]

In this ideological struggle, the media has become the prime battleground for influencing the votes and minds of Americans. We see Fox News taking on the role of the nation's conservative conscience while mainstream newspapers such as the *New York Times* and the *Los Angeles Times* often reflect Democratic positions. This helps explain why many of the Canada-bashing comments since the September 11 attacks in 2001 have come from the likes of Tucker Carlson, Ann Coulter, and Bill O'Reilly. For in many conservative circles, Canada is the prime example of what *not* to become. What would happen if the United States brought in universal health care? Look at Canada with wait times so long citizens are crossing *into* the United States to pay cash for care. What would happen if the United States expanded its social programs? Look at Canada where taxes are so high those with ambition pack their suitcases and run to Lady Liberty (or to Alberta). Of course, this is an exaggeration, but the point is still there. From defence to health care and a host of other social welfare services, Canada is a living, breathing example of a North American country sans unbridled capitalism. So while some blue-blooded journalists muse of Canada as utopia, others in the conservative media see it as a mediocre hell.

What then can be predicted of future American media coverage on Canada–U.S. relations? One could reasonably presume that the election of a Democratic president whose philosophies align more closely with Canadian policies would bode well for relations and positive news coverage about Canada, at least in "liberal" media circles. Of course, among "conservative" outlets the Canada bashing may continue as the administration's policies on issues such as health care and education are criticized.

In 2008, as Senator Barack Obama ran for the presidency, his action plan to pull the United States out of its recession raised concerns of possible anti-Canadian sentiment and caused some early hiccups in bilateral relations. During the Democratic primaries, Obama's anti-NAFTA remarks were widely publicized in both countries. While Obama was attempting to grab the votes of middle-class Americans hit by job losses in the manufacturing sector, it could be argued there was an ever-so-faint whiff of anti-Canadianism in his statements, whether deliberate or not.[20] For if the United States were to edge toward protectionism — as Congress did in the February 2009 federal stimulus package which included a "Buy American" provision for steel, iron, and other manufactured goods used in public works projects — any resulting policies would inevitably affect the massive cross-border trade relationship with Canada. That's why the Canadian government, along with the European Union and prominent American corporations, lobbied heavily for a caveat in the stimulus bill to clarify that "Buy American" couldn't violate international trade agreements.

Looking at the media industry itself, there's the decline and subsequent slow growth in audience for Fox News in 2006 and 2007 to consider. These developments have led to speculation that the cable news network may have associated itself too closely with the Bush administration and a Republican agenda, and lost viewers as America tilted left heading into the 2008 election.[21] If this trend continues and Fox News shuffles shows or attempts to remake its image, this could mean a drop in the amount of Canada bashing heard on the network. Also, as President Obama champions socialist solutions to fix societal ills, conservative commentators may shift their attacks from Canada to the president and his administration.

Or the future could hold more Canada-bashing comments. From Confederation onward, waves of anti-Canadianism in the American media correlate with periods when major government policies differed between the two countries. That trend, no matter how great relations seem at the present, can be expected to continue, in spite of, or perhaps because of, ever-increasing bilateral interconnectedness.

Either way, one thing is certain — the coming decades will see less comprehensive coverage of Canada in the American media. Gone are correspondents like the *New York Times*' Jay Walz, the *Chicago Tribune*'s Eugene Griffin, and the *Los Angeles Times*' Stanley Meisler. In 2007, the *Washington Post* shuttered its Canadian bureau, following in the footsteps of other American media outlets, including the *New York Times*, the *Los Angeles Times*, and the *Wall Street Journal*. A few American wire correspondents were left to pick up the slack. While the *Post*'s foreign news manager said at the time that the paper planned to continue and possibly increase its coverage of Canada, a CBC News article noted what had happened at the *New York Times*. In the year after the *Times* closed its bureau, the CBC reported that the average number of feature-length articles about Canada decreased by 23 percent.[22] Why? Wire correspondents cover breaking news, leaving the feature stories and analysis for other journalists. As there are no more Canada-based journalists daily pitching ideas to their foreign desk editors at major newspapers, there's simply less coverage. It's hard to rely on freelancers who send sporadic pitches, or beat reporters and correspondents based in the United States. That would be like having a journalist in Los Angeles covering a story in Mexico City. You can make all the phone calls you want, but without living there, you miss the nuances, the talk on the street, the information from cultivated sources. In the end, it's a vicious cycle. Reduced coverage of Canada means fewer Americans will know or care about the country, which will result in even fewer stories about it.

A dearth of Canadian correspondents will also ultimately result in Americans having greater misconceptions and minimal general knowledge about their northern neighbour. Take a second and ponder this — how much do you really know about Mexico? Japan? Germany? Can you name the head of their governments? All of these nations are major trading partners with the United States, yet stereotypes abound. Canada, trumping each of these countries when it comes to a trade partnership with the U.S., suffers from the same American apathy. And when a major story breaks in Canada — as it is guaranteed to at some point — there will be no correspondents there to cover it. Sure, American reporters may be flown in or write about it from their desks, but the coverage will be basic, lacking in the depth and knowledge that's gained by living in a country and understanding both Canadian and American concerns. At that point, who will be left to defend Canada?

★★★ **NOTES** ★★★

CHAPTER 1
The First Five Years: 1867–1872

[1] Psalm 72:8 is the verse MP Samuel Tilley is believed to have drawn inspiration from when suggesting the name "Dominion" for Canada.

[2] Of the five prominent national newspapers quoted extensively in this book, the *Chicago Tribune* and the *New York Times* were the only papers in print at this time.

[3] "Afraid of Canada," *Chicago Tribune*, March 1, 1867.

[4] Ibid.

[5] "Canadian Royalty," *Chicago Tribune*, March 5, 1867.

[6] Ibid.

[7] From Our Own Correspondent, "Canada," *New York Times*, March 6, 1867, 2.

[8] "A Standing Army for British American and Its Cost," *New York Times*, May 23, 1867, 4.

[9] Ibid.

[10] "The Kingdom of Canada," *Chicago Tribune*, February 28, 1867.

[11] "The War Against Thistles," *Chicago Tribune*, November 20, 1871, 4.

[12] "The Canada Thistle," *Chicago Tribune*, April 13, 1867.

[13] "The Fire in the Woods in Canada," *New York Times*, August 11, 1868, 1.

[14] "The Canadian Flurry," *New York Times*, March 10, 1866, 4.

[15] "The Fenian Collapse," *Chicago Tribune*, June 4, 1866.

[16] "The Fenian Folly," *Chicago Tribune*, May 26, 1870.

[17] "The Fenian Campaign," *Chicago Tribune*, May 27, 1870.

[18] "The Fizzle in Vermont," *Chicago Tribune*, May 30, 1870.

[19] "The Latest News from Canada," *New York Times*, May 26, 1870, 4.

[20]   "Wanted, a Colonial Policy," *New York Times*, February 16, 1870, 4.

[21]   "Annexation – British Columbia – Nova Scotia," *Chicago Tribune*, December 2, 1867.

[22]   Ibid.

[23]   "A Foolish Project to Take the Canadas by Force," *New York Times*, January 4, 1869, 5.

[24]   Ibid.

[25]   Joseph Medill, "An Ocean-Bound Republic," *New York Times*, January 26, 1869, 2.

[26]   "What Canada Thinks of Mr. Medill's Proposition to Take the Dominion," *New York Times*, February 1, 1869, 2.

[27]   "...And the Alabama Claims," *Chicago Tribune*, April 21, 1869.

[28]   Ibid.

[29]   See note 27 above.

[30]   "American and Canadian Union," *Chicago Tribune*, September 3, 1870.

[31]   "Canadian Annexation," *Chicago Tribune*, November 19, 1870.

[32]   "Canadian Independence," *Chicago Tribune*, January 4, 1870.

[33]   "The Canadian Bother," *Chicago Tribune*, January 25, 1868.

[34]   "The Canadian Exodus," *Chicago Tribune*, April 1, 1869.

[35]   John Herd Thompson and Mark Paul Richard, "Canadian History in North American Context," in *Canadian Studies in the New Millennium*, ed. Patrick James and Mark Kasoff (Toronto: University of Toronto Press, 2008), 50.

[36]   See note 33 above.

[37]   Ibid.

[38]   Thompson and Richard, "Canadian History in North American Context," 50.

[39]   "Canada," *New York Times*, December 21, 1872, 9.

[40]   "British North America," *New York Times*, April 14, 1869, 1.

[41]   Ibid.

[42]   See note 34 above.

CHAPTER 2
Free Trade or "Freedom": 1911

1   Quoted by the *Chicago Tribune*, June 4, 1911.

2   "Effect of Reciprocity," *Los Angeles Times*, March 25, 1911, 114.

3   "Canadian Cabinet Visits US in Force," *New York Times*, January 7, 1911, 6.

4   "Canada and the United States," *New York Times*, January 8, 1911, AFR30.

5   Ibid.

6   "Canada's Dilemma," *Washington Post*, January 13, 1911, 6.

.7   "Would Keep Trade Bars Up," *Washington Post*, January 10, 1911, 12.

8   "The Canadian Agreement," *Chicago Tribune*, January 28, 1911, 10.

9   "The Selfish Farmers," *Washington Post*, January 31, 1911, 6.

10   Ibid.

11   "Oddities of Reciprocity," *Washington Post*, February 1, 1911, 6.

12   "The Real Issue of Reciprocity," *Chicago Tribune*, February 10, 1911, 10.

13   Ibid.

14   "Breaking Down the Barriers, and Developing the Northwest," *Wall Street Journal*, February 11, 1911, 6.

15   "Reciprocity Wins," *Washington Post*, February 15, 1911, 1.

16   "Democrats and Annexation," *Washington Post*, February 16, 1911, 6.

17   Ibid.

18   "Don't be Jocose," *Chicago Tribune*, February 17, 1911, 8.

19   "Taboos Annexation Plans," *Washington Post*, February 18, 1911, 4.

20   "Would Annex Canada," *Washington Post*, February 17, 1911, 3; Direct Wire to the Times, "Annex Canada, Says Bennett [sic]," *Los Angeles Times*, February 17, 1911, I1; Kendrick A. Clements, "Manifest Destiny and Canadian Reciprocity in 1911," *Pacific Historical Review*, Vol. 42, No. 1 (February 1973): 38.

21   "Canada is Bunkoed," *Washington Post*, February 17, 1911, 1.

22 Ibid.

23 "Asks Laurier to Defeat It," *Los Angeles Times*,
    February 18, 1911, I17.

24 "Reciprocity," *Los Angeles Times*, March 6, 1911, 16.

25 "It's Different in Canada," *Washington Post*, February 17,
    1911, 6.

26 "President Urges Reciprocity Act," *Chicago Tribune*,
    April 6, 1911, 7.

27 "Bringing Canada Nearer," *New York Times*, June 25,
    1911, 10.

28 "Now or Never," *Chicago Tribune*, May 14, 1911, B4.

29 "The Crux of Reciprocity," *Washington Post*, July 6, 1911, 6.

30 "Reciprocity and California," *Los Angeles Times*, April 15,
    1911, I14.

31 Walter J. Ballard, "Reciprocity with Canada," *Los Angeles
    Times*, April 6, 1911, I14.

32 Ibid.

33 "Canadian 'Reciprocity' not Reciprocal," *Los Angeles
    Times*, July 5, 1911, I14.

34 "The 'Colossus,'" *Los Angeles Times*, June 12, 1911, I14.

35 Ibid.

36 "A Canuck Booster," *Los Angeles Times*, June 10, 1911, I14.

37 "Annexation Peril Anti-Laurier Cry," *New York Times*,
    July 31, 1911, 1.

38 "Reciprocity's Prospects," *New York Times*, July 22, 1911, 6.

39 "Exciting Times in Canada," *Washington Post*, July 27,
    1911, 6.

40 "Fear Political Riots," *Los Angeles Times*, June 25, 1911, 13.

41 See note 39 above.

42 "Annexation Peril is Seen by Borden," *New York Times*,
    August 16, 1911, 7.

43 "A False Statement," *Chicago Tribune*, August 16, 1911, 10.

44 "One Issue in Canada," *Washington Post*, August 21,
    1911, 8; "Drop Muckraking in Canada," *Chicago Tribune*,
    August 21, 1911, 11.

45 "Taft in the Canadian Campaign," *Washington Post*,
    September 19, 1911, 6; "Both Sides Claim Canadian Victory
    in Voting Today," *Chicago Tribune*, September 21, 1911, 1.

46   "Calamity Cries from Canada," *Los Angeles Times*,
     September 7, 1911, I4.

47   "A Touch of Comedy," *Chicago Tribune*, September 2,
     1911, 8.

48   John Callan O'Laughlin, "Canadians Need United States as
     Aid to Commerce," *Chicago Tribune*, September 11, 1911, 1.

49   John Callan O'Laughlin, "Politics Played in Treaty Fight,"
     Chicago Tribune, September 17, 1911, A1.

50   "Canadians Pick Laurier to Win," *Los Angeles Times*,
     September 17, 1911, I4.

51   "Taft in the Canadian Campaign," *Washington Post*,
     September 19, 1911, 6.

52   Ibid.

53   Before the election, Borden's Conservatives had 85
     seats and Laurier's Liberals had 133 seats. With a shift
     of about 3 percent in the popular vote the map of
     Parliament reversed, with the Conservatives winning 132
     seats (48.56% popular vote, up 2.34%) and the Liberals
     winning 85 seats (45.82% popular vote, down 3.05%).

54   "President Taft Disappointed," *New York Times*,
     September 22, 1911, 1.

55   "Used Clark's Speech," *New York Times*, September 22,
     1911, 2.

56   "Defeat of Reciprocity," *Washington Post*, September 22,
     1911, 6.

57   "Canada's Verdict," *Chicago Tribune*, September 23, 1911, 8.

58   "A Disappointment and its Consequences," *Wall Street
     Journal*, September 23, 1911, 1.

59   "The Canadian Surprise," *New York Times*, September 23,
     1911, 6.

60   "The Bogy Laid," *Los Angeles Times*, September 24, 1911, I4.

61   W.S.G., "The Canadian Vote," *New York Times*,
     September 26, 1911, 8.

62   Tom MacRae, "Why Canada Declined," *Chicago Tribune*,
     September 29, 1911, 8.

63   "Just Because," *Los Angeles Times*, October 1, 1911, I4.

CHAPTER 3
Castro, Nukes & the Cold War: 1953–1968

[1]   *New York Times*, September 19, 1966.
[2]   Thompson and Richard, "Canadian History in North American Context," 56.
[3]   Richard H. Parke, "Canada Moves Resolutely to Aid Western Defense," *New York Times*, February 13, 1951, 1.
[4]   Ibid.
[5]   Warren Unna, "Envoy Kills Himself; Canada Blames U.S.," *Washington Post*, April 5, 1957, A1.
[6]   "Put Out the Fire," *Washington Post*, April 11, 1957, A26.
[7]   Philip Deane, "Canada-US: Inevitable Allies," *New Republic*, April 29, 1957, 9–10.
[8]   "Canada OK's Hike in Trade with Cubans," *Chicago Tribune*, December 10, 1960, 4.
[9]   "Opposition Party Backs Canada on Cuba Trade," *Los Angeles Times*, December 12, 1960, 6.
[10] "Headed Apart, Hand in Hand," *Chicago Tribune*, December 17, 1960, B14.
[11] Rowland Evans Jr., "Time of Vast, Varied Change in U.S. Dawns," *Los Angeles Times*, January 1, 1961, 12.
[12] George E. Sokolsky, "These Days," *Washington Post*, August 25, 1961, A15.
[13] Ibid.
[14] Charles A. Cooper, "Trading with the Communists," *New Republic*, October 12, 1963, 9–12.
[15] Harry Trimborn, "Canadians Approve of Wheat Sales to Reds," *Los Angeles Times*, July 18, 1966, 4.
[16] Ibid.
[17] Robert S. Allen and Paul Scott, "Cuba Blockade to Keep on Leaking," *Los Angeles Times*, February 27, 1964, A5.
[18] "Who's Isolating Whom?" *Chicago Tribune*, January 9, 1964, 16.
[19] Allen and Scott, A5.
[20] "Our Allies, So-Called," *Chicago Tribune*, July 30, 1967, 20.
[21] "Forgotten Country?" *New York Times*, June 11, 1958, 34.
[22] G.V. Ferguson, "It's a Step, At Least, in Dual Defense," *Washington Post*, June 7, 1959, E5.

23   George Gallup, "Gallup Poll," *Los Angeles Times,*
     December 1, 1961, 11.

24   Associated Press, "14,000 Idled as Canada Junks Its Jet
     Program," *Washington Post,* February 22, 1959, A21.

25   Raymond Daniell, "Canada Abandons Military Jet Plan,"
     New York Times, February 21, 1959, 3.

26   Associated Press, "Action is Scored," *New York Times,*
     February 21, 1959, 3.

27   Eugene Griffin, "Canada Hikes Demands for U.S.
     Business," *Chicago Tribune,* February 26, 1959, A3.

28   Ibid.

29   G.V. Ferguson, "Nuclear Aspects of Sovereignty,"
     Washington Post, January 31, 1960, E2.

30   Marquis Childs, "New Isolationism After the Crisis,"
     Washington Post, February 13, 1963, A16.

31   Ibid.

32   "Losing Friends Fast," *Chicago Tribune,* February 2, 1963, 12.

33   Warren Duffee, "Morse Defends U.S. on Canada
     Dispute," *Washington Post,* February 10, 1963, A14.

34   "The Canadian Tempest," *Washington Post,*
     February 2, 1963, A8.

35   "The Storm from Canada," *New York Times,* February 4,
     1963, 6.

36   "The World: Canadian Storm," *New York Times,*
     February 4, 1963, 9.

37   See note 35 above.

38   See note 32 above.

39   "Canadian Fuss: Sadly Necessary," *Los Angeles Times,*
     February 4, 1963, A4.

40   Ibid.

41   Max Freedman, "Rebuke of Canada Defense Policy
     Called Profound U.S. Blunder," *Los Angeles Times,*
     February 5, 1963, A5.

42   Max Freedman, "In Perspective: The Quarrel with
     Canada – II," *Washington Post,* February 4, 1963, A15.

43   "The U.S.A. and Canada," *New York Times,* February 7,
     1963, 5.

44   Harlan S. Byrne, "Crisis in Canada," *Wall Street Journal*, February 12, 1963, 1.

45   Ibid.

46   Drew Pearson, "Closer U.S.–Canada Ties Needed," *Washington Post*, February 10, 1963, E7.

47   "Diefenbaker Wants No Atom 'Dump' in Canada," *Los Angeles Times*, March 4, 1963, 11; "Canadian Would Bar A-Arms Short of Crisis," *Washington Post*, March 4, 1963, A16.

48   Harlan S. Byrne, "Canada's Election," *Wall Street Journal*, March 27, 1963, 1.

49   Samuel Lubell, "The People Speak," *Los Angeles Times*, March 28, 1963, 17.

50   Ibid.

51   Drew Pearson, "Canadians are Basically Pro-U.S.," *Washington Post*, April 8, 1963, B23.

52   "Canada's New Course," *New York Times*, May 7, 1963, 42.

53   "Canada's Nuclear Decision," *New York Times*, May 14, 1963, 36.

54   "Muddying the Waters," *Chicago Tribune*, February 12, 1965, 16.

55   Ibid.

56   Associated Press, "Canadian Leader Asks 'Pause' in Viet Strikes," *Los Angeles Times*, April 3, 1965, 14.

57   William G. Weart, "Air Strike Pause Urged by Pearson," *New York Times*, April 3, 1965, 3.

58   Laurence Stern, "Leaders Hold Conference at Camp David," *Washington Post*, April 4, 1965, A1. Also: Cabell Phillips, "President is Cool to Pearson Plan," *New York Times*, April 4, 1965, 1.

59   Robert E. Thompson, "Johnson Remains Silent on 'Pause' in Bombing," *Los Angeles Times*, April 4, 1965, 1.

60   Ibid.

61   Jay Walz, "U.S. Irks Canada by Vietnam Move," *New York Times*, May 23, 1965, 36.

62   "Pearson's Flip-Flop," *Chicago Tribune*, April 7, 1965, 20.

63   Reuters, "Tells Canada's Stand on U.S. in Viet Nam," *Chicago Tribune*, May 8, 1965, S2.

64   See note 61 above.

65   Ibid.

66   "Reservations in Ottawa," *New York Times*, July 13, 1965, 14.

67   Ibid.

68   Vermont Royster, "Thinking Things Over," *Wall Street Journal*, June 2, 1965, 14.

69   John M. Lee, "Canada Proves to be a Haven for Draft Dodgers from U.S.," *New York Times*, September 15, 1966, 8; Oliver Clausen, "Boys Without a Country," *New York Times*, May 21, 1967, SM25.

70   Lansing R. Shepard, "Some U.S. Draft Evaders Plan to Remain in Canada," *Christian Science Monitor*, December 26, 1968, 3.

71   CBC News Online, "Draft-Dodger Memorial to be Built in B.C.," cbcnews.ca, September 8, 2004, http://www.cbc.ca/story/canada/national/2004/09/08/draft_dogers040908.html (accessed May 6, 2008).

72   Louis B. Fleming, "Canadian Plan for Viet Peace Endorsed by U.S.," *Los Angeles Times*, March 29, 1966, 1.

73   "U.S. Statement on Vietnam," *New York Times*, April 20, 1967, 2.

74   Harry Trimborn, "Canada–U.S. Tieup? Some Other Time!" *Los Angeles Times*, August 28, 1966, J2.

75   "Unhelpful Allies," *Chicago Tribune*, March 3, 1967, 20.

76   Jay Walz, "Canada, in her Centennial Year, Weighs the Future," *New York Times*, January 2, 1967, 1.

77   Ibid.

78   Marquis Childs, "Canada's Temper on an Anniversary," *Washington Post*, February 22, 1967, A24.

79   Ibid.

CHAPTER 4
Enter the Intellect: 1968–1984

1   Robert Prinsky, "Dark-Horse Bachelor from Quebec Gaining in his Drive to be Canada's Prime Minister," *Wall Street Journal*, February 5, 1968, 7.

2   Robert H. Estabrook, "Dazzling Contender for Canada's Helm," *Washington Post*, March 31, 1968, B1.

3   Alex Campbell, "Canada's Future," *New Republic*, March 9, 1968, 15-16.

4   Ibid.

5   Frank Flaherty, "Trudeau: Monsieur Playboy," *Washington Post*, April 28, 1968, K11.

6   Jay Walz, "Canada: Trudeau's Gamble," *New York Times*, April 28, 1968, E11.

7   George Bain, "Canada has a Case of Trudeaumania," *New York Times*, June 16, 1968, SM10.

8   Ibid.

9   "Canada's Kennedy," *Chicago Tribune*, June 27, 1968, 20.

10   Ibid.

11   "Canada Opts for Change," *New York Times*, June 27, 1968, 42.

12   Ibid.

13   Richard Homan, "Canadians Opt for 'Pop' Premier," *Washington Post*, June 28, 1968, A20.

14   "Canada's Next Prime Minister Pierre Elliott Trudeau," *New York Times*, April 8, 1968, 8.

15   See note 13 above.

16   Max Lerner, "Canada Shows Time is Ripe to Elect a Swinging Leader," *Los Angeles Times*, June 28, 1968, B5.

17   Dorothy McCardle, "Bachelor 'PM' Coming to Dinner," *Washington Post*, March 24, 1969, D2.

18   Margaret Crimmins, "Trudeau's Swinger Image Tarnished by Appearance," *Los Angeles Times*, March 28, 1969, J14.

19   "Canada's Independent Stance," *Los Angeles Times*, March 27, 1969, E6.

20   James Reston, "Washington: Will Canada Leave the North Atlantic Alliance?" *New York Times*, March 28, 1969, 46.

21   Eugene Griffin, "Self-Interest: A Canadian Mood Study," *Chicago Tribune*, June 15, 1969, 1.

22   Edward Cowan, "Economic Ties to U.S. Arouse Canadian Fears," *New York Times*, January 19, 1970, 75.

23   Peter Thomson, "Canada's Claims in Arctic Add to Strains with U.S.," *Los Angeles Times*, April 27, 1970, A9.

24 Jay Walz, "Trudeau Beset by Old Problems," *New York Times*, April 13, 1970, 6.

25 "Canada on Guard," *Chicago Tribune*, October 17, 1970, S10.

26 Benjamin Welles, "U.S. Use of Sweeping Powers is Doubted," *New York Times*, October 17, 1970, 13.

27 Eugene Griffin, "Trudeau, Canada Gain New Stature in Response to Crisis," *Chicago Tribune*, October 25, 1970, 1.

28 "Trudeau's Courage...," *Christian Science Monitor*, October 28, 1970, 14.

29 Claude Lemelin, "Canada: Our Furious Friend," *Washington Post*, October 24, 1971, 89.

30 "Trudeau Warns U.S. on Economy," *Chicago Tribune*, September 24, 1971, 10.

31 James Bassett, "Canada Deeply Offended as 'Best Friend' Puts up Fence," *Los Angeles Times*, October 3, 1971, G1.

32 "Canada: A Special Relationship," *Christian Science Monitor*, October 9, 1971, 18.

33 "Do We Care About Canada?" *New York Times*, November 7, 1971, E10.

34 Murray Seeger, "Canada: Rumblings from '51st State' Grow Louder," *Los Angeles Times*, October 24, 1971, F1.

35 Ibid.

36 "Do We Care About Canada?" *New York Times*, November 7, 1971, E10.

37 James Reston, "The Bad Neighbor Policy," *New York Times*, December 12, 1971, E11.

38 Robert B. Semple Jr., "Nixon, in Ottawa, Asks Recognition of Differences," *New York Times*, April 15, 1972, 1. Also: Anthony Astrachan, "Canada Gets U.S. Pledge," *Washington Post*, April 15, 1972, A1.

39 "Trauma in Canada," *Wall Street Journal*, April 17, 1972, 16.

40 George F. Will, "The Canadian Soul," *Washington Post*, January 4, 1976, 111.

41 Ibid.

42 Eugene Griffin, "Quebec Seeks More Power from Canada," *Chicago Tribune*, February 18, 1968, A1.

43   "Trudeau Program Attacked," *Washington Post*, January 12, 1976, C7.

44   "Canada's Man in Havana," *New York Times*, January 31, 1976, 19.

45   Ibid.

46   "Trudeau on Castro," *Chicago Tribune*, February 3, 1976, A2.

47   Robert Lewis, "Trudeau in Cuba: Blue Jeans, Frisbees and Fidel," *Washington Post*, February 13, 1976, B9.

48   Ysabel Trujillo, "The Trudeau Era is Over for Canada's Angry Voters," *Chicago Tribune*, October 21, 1978, W12.

49   "The Canadian Dollar," *Wall Street Journal*, August 3, 1977, 10.

50   Stanley Meisler, "Testing Time Growing Nigh for Trudeau," *Los Angeles Times*, February 1, 1979, A5.

51   "Au Revoir, Pierre," *Chicago Tribune*, November 24, 1979, S8.

52   Stanley Meisler, "Caller Indicated Growing Danger for 6 in Tehran," *Los Angeles Times*, February 2, 1980, A1.

53   "O, Canada!" *Washington Post*, January 31, 1980, A20.

54   Ibid.

55   "Canadian caper," *Christian Science Monitor*, January 31, 1980, 24.

56   Ibid.

57   Charles Carney, "County Says Thank You for a Neighborly Deed," *Los Angeles Times*, February 11, 1980, OC_A10.

58   David A. Andelman, "Canadians Are Suddenly Heroes, And Americans Extend Thanks," *New York Times*, February 2, 1980, 1.

59   "Canadian Flag to Fly at City Hall," *Los Angeles Times*, February 2, 1980, A7. Also, David A. Andelman, "Canadians Are Suddenly Heroes, And Americans Extend Thanks," *New York Times*, February 2, 1980, 1.

60   Ibid.

61   Mary McGrory, "An Ode to a Good Neighbor," *Chicago Tribune*, February 6, 1980, E3.

62   Ibid.

63   "Ottawa's Example," *Wall Street Journal*, February 1, 1980, 16.

64   Dusko Doder, "Trudeau Hints at Looser Ties to
     Washington," *Washington Post*, February 20, 1980, A1.

65   "Welcoming Mr. Trudeau," *Wall Street Journal*, July 9,
     1981, 24.

66   "The Canadian Disease," *Wall Street Journal*, March 9,
     1981, 22.

67   "Canada Says Nationalization not Anti-American
     Program," *Washington Post*, August 9, 1981, F1.

68   George Skelton, "Reagan Warns Trudeau Over Energy
     Policy," *Los Angeles Times*, September 18, 1981, OC1.

69   "Get Canada Off the Back Burner," *Chicago Tribune*,
     September 29, 1981, 20.

70   "Clouds on the Border," *Christian Science Monitor*,
     October 13, 1981, 28.

71   "Canadian Quarrel," *Washington Post*, October 3, 1981, A22.

72   Stanley Meisler, "Canada's Trudeau: Sexy, Brilliant,
     Arrogant and an Enduring Engima," *Los Angeles Times*,
     July 11, 1982, F2.

73   Andy Stark, "Pierre Trudeau's 15 Years of Failure," *Wall
     Street Journal*, April 12, 1983, 34.

74   Ibid.

75   John Urquhart and Frederick Rose, "Canada's Trudeau
     Says He Will Resign As Prime Minister, Seen Leaving by
     July," *Wall Street Journal*, March 1, 1984, 2.

76   Kenneth Freed, "Canada's Retiring World Diplomat Still
     Gets Almost No Respect at Home," *Los Angeles Times*,
     March 11, 1984, E2.

77   Lansing Lamont, "Canada's Relations With Us," *The New
     York Times*, July 6, 1984, A23.

78   "Big Doings in Canada," *Los Angeles Times*, July 12, 1984,
     D6.

79   "Canada's Non-Choice," *Wall Street Journal*, August 28,
     1984, 26.

80   Janet Cawley, "Patience pays off for Mulroney," *Chicago
     Tribune*, September 5, 1984, 2.

81   "Canada Turns Right," *The New York Times*, September 6,
     1984, A22.

[82] "Good news from Canada," *Chicago Tribune*, September 7, 1984, 26.

[83] Kenneth Freed, "Mulroney the 'Conservative': It's Different in Canada," *Los Angeles Times*, September 9, 1984, D2.

CHAPTER 5
Hitting Below the Belt: 2001 Onward

[1] Embassy of Canada, Washington, "The Canada–U.S. Trade and Investment Partnership," Government of Canada, http://geo.international.gc.ca/can-am/washington/trade_and_investment/trade_partnership-en.asp (accessed May 22, 2008).

[2] Embassy of Canada, Washington, "Oil," Foreign Affairs and International Trade Canada, http://geo.international.gc.ca/can-am/main/right_nav/oil-en.asp (accessed May 22, 2008).

[3] Embassy of Canada, Washington, "Natural Gas," Foreign Affairs and International Trade Canada, http://geo.international.gc.ca/can-am/main/right_nav/natural_gas-en.asp (accessed May 22, 2008).

[4] "Canada's Actions Against Terrorism Since September 11," Foreign Affairs and International Trade Canada, http://www.dfait-maeci.gc.ca/anti-terrorism/Canadaactions-en.asp (accessed January 15, 2009).

[5] Kathy Borrus, "A New Perspective, Courtesy of Newfoundland Samaritans," *Washington Post*, September 18, 2001, C10.

[6] Marian Osher, "Canadians' Hospitality Sweet," *Washington Post*, September 27, 2001, T04.

[7] "The Neighbors," *New York Times*, September 22, 2001, B3.

[8] Dan Eggen, "FBI Launches Massive Manhunt; Hijackers Trained As Pilots in U.S.," *Washington Post*, September 13, 2001, A01.

[9] DeNeen L. Brown and Ceci Connolly, "Suspects Entered Easily From Canada; Authorities Scrutinize Border Posts in Maine," *Washington Post*, September 14, 2001, A17.

10   Barbara Crossette, "U.S. Seeks Canada's Reassurance on
      Security," *New York Times*, September 14, 2001, A21.

11   See note 9 above. Also: DeNeen L. Brown, "Attacks
      Force Canadians To Face Their Own Threat; Intelligence
      Agents Identify More Than 50 Suspect Groups,"
      Washington Post, September 23, 2001, A36. Dan Eggen,
      "U.S. Plans Stronger Border Security; Guard Troops
      Would Help Monitor Entry Ports From Canada,"
      Washington Post, December 2, 2001, A14.

12   "A Border in Sharper Focus," *Los Angeles Times*,
      September 26, 2001, B12.

13   Ibid.

14   Barbara Crossette, "Chrétien Under Pressure From Right
      and Left Over What to Give Washington," *New York
      Times*, September 23, 2001, B7.

15   DeNeen L. Brown, "Canadians Sense Climate of Fear;
      Some Say Living Next to U.S. Creates Unaccustomed
      Threat," *Washington Post*, October 24, 2001, A06.

16   Ipsos-Reid, "Seven-in-Ten (72%) Canadians Support U.S.
      Led Air Strikes on Terrorist Targets in Afghanistan,"
      October 15, 2001.

17   Robert Stasko, "Canada's Fallen Soldiers," *Washington
      Post*, April 23, 2002, A16.

18   "Best Friends, Like It or Not," *Los Angeles Times*, April 27,
      2002, B24.

19   Clifford Krauss, "Canadian Families Split on Fate of U.S.
      Pilots," *New York Times*, February 9, 2003, L4.

20   David E. Sanger, "Bush Asks Leaders in 3 Key Nations for
      Iraq Support," *New York Times*, September 7, 2002, A1.

21   Jonah Goldberg, "Soviet Canuckistan," *National Review
      Online*, November 8, 2002.

22   Jonah Goldberg, "Bomb Canada: The Case for War,"
      National Review, November 25, 2002, 30-32.

23   Ibid.

24   See note 22 above.

25 DeNeen L. Brown, "Aide to Chretien Quits in Flap Over Gibe About Bush," *Washington Post*, November 27, 2002, A14. Also: Reuters, "Canadian Government Aide Who Called Bush a 'Moron' Resigns," *New York Times*, November 27, 2002, A6.

26 DeNeen L. Brown, "Canadian Apologizes for Expletive About U.S.," *Washington Post*, February 28, 2003, A17.

27 Al Kamen, "Escalation of the Appellation," *Washington Post*, February 28, 2003, A21.

28 Ian Austen, "In Canada, Acting Out Contempt for Bush and his Policies Wasn't Viewed as Funny," *New York Times*, November 22, 2004, C6.

29 Richard W. Stevenson and David E. Sanger, "U.S Resisting Calls For a 2nd U.N. Vote On a War With Iraq," *New York Times*, January 16, 2003, A1.

30 Nicholas D. Kristof, "Losses, Before Bullets Fly," *New York Times*, March 7, 2003, A27.

31 Ibid.

32 Dan Mihalopoulos, "Some Canadians fear for U.S. ties; Anti-war stance may have fallout," *Chicago Tribune*, April 9, 2003, 7.

33 DeNeen L. Brown, "Chretien Tells Canadians To Respect U.S. Decision; Leader Tries to Curb Anti-American Sentiment," *Washington Post*, March 21, 2003, A29.

34 See note 32 above.

35 Ibid.

36 Clifford Krauss, "In Canada, Tourism Is Easing Its Way Back," *New York Times*, May 30, 2004, TR3.

37 CBC News Online, "Timeline of BSE in Canada and the U.S.," cbcnews.ca, October 23, 2006, http://www.cbc.ca/news/background/madcow/timeline.html (accessed January 20, 2009).

38 Kevin J. Christiano, "Woe, Canada? Things not so bad," *Chicago Tribune*, June 8, 2003, 3.

39 Clifford Krauss, "Canada's View on Social Issues Is Opening Rifts With the U.S.," *New York Times*, December 2, 2003, A1.

40 David Montgomery, "Whoa! Canada! Legal Marijuana.
Gay Marriage. Peace. What the Heck's Going on up
North, Eh?" *Washington Post*, July 1, 2003, C01.

41 Matt Labash, "Welcome to Canada: The Great White
Waste of Time," *Weekly Standard*, 10.25, March 21,
2005, 23–29.

42 Ibid.

43 John Gibson, "Un-Happy Birthday, Canada," *Maclean's*,
July 1, 2005, 25.

44 CBC News Online, "Anti-Bush protesters scuffle with
police," cbcnews.ca, December 1, 2004, http://www.cbc.
ca/canada/story/2004/11/30/bush_arrives041130.html
(accessed February 1, 2009).

45 Tucker Carlson, Media Matters for America, November
30, 2004, http://mediamatters.org/items/200412010011
(accessed May 23, 2008).

46 Tucker Carlson, Transcript, CNN *Crossfire*,
November 30, 2004, http://transcripts.cnn.com/
TRANSCRIPTS/0411/30/cf.01.html (accessed
May 23, 2008).

47 Ann Coulter, Media Matters for America, November 30,
2004, http://mediamatters.org/items/200412010011
(accessed May 23, 2008).

48 Clifford Krauss, "Canada May Be Close Neighbor, but It
Proudly Keeps Its Distance," *New York Times*, March 23,
2005, A8.

49 Ibid.

50 CBC News Online, "Martin rejects U.S. ambassador's
rebuke," cbcnews.ca, December 13, 2005, http://www.
cbc.ca/story/canadavotes2006/national/2005/12/13/
wilkins-051213.html (accessed May 11, 2009).

51 Tucker Carlson, Media Matters for America, December
16, 2005, http://mediamatters.org/items/200512160012
(accessed May 23, 2008).

52 Ibid (accessed May 23, 2008).

53 Neil Cavuto, Media Matters for America, December 14,
2005 (posted 16 December), http://mediamatters.org/
items/200512160008 (accessed May 23, 2008).

54   Ibid.

55   Douglas MacKinnon, "Oh, no, Canada: America can no Longer Look the Other Way," *Washington Times*, December 16, 2005, A23.

56   Ibid.

57   John Gibson, "The O'Reilly Factor," Fox News Network, April 12, 2004, http://w3.nexis.com:80/new/search/homesubmitForm.do (accessed through Nexis, May 23, 2008).

58   Bill O'Reilly, Media Matters for America, February 24, 2006, http://mediamatters.org/items/200602240004 (accessed May 23, 2008).

59   David Owen, "Penny Dreadful," *New Yorker*, March 31, 2008, 66.

EPILOGUE

1   Lydia Saad, "China Down, France up in Americans' Ratings," Gallup, March 3, 2008, http://www.gallup.com/poll/104719/China-Down-France-Americans-Ratings.aspx (accessed May 29, 2008).

2   Guy Michaels and Xiaojia Zhi, "Freedom Fries," CEP Discussion Paper No 815, London School of Economics and Political Science, July 2007, 17.

3   "Country Ratings," Gallup, http://www.gallup.com/poll/1624/Perceptions-Foreign-Countries.aspx (accessed March 30, 2009).

4   "Pew Global Attitudes Project: Spring 2005 Survey: Final Topline," Pew Research Center for the People and the Press, Spring 2005, 7.

5   "Americans and Canadians: The North American Not-so-Odd Couple," Pew Research Center for the People and the Press, January 14, 2004, http://peoplepress.org/commentary/print.php3?AnalysisID=80 (accessed May 22, 2008).

6   "Canadians' Perceptions and Attitudes Towards
    the United States," The Strategic Counsel, March
    27, 2006, [http://www.thestrategiccounsel.com/
    our_news/polls/2006-03-27%20GMCTV%20Mar25-
    26%20(Mar27).pdf] (accessed May 22, 2008).

7   Ibid.

8   "A Tale of Two Nations; State of Canadian/American
    Public Opinion," The Strategic Counsel, June 2008,
    [http://www.thestrategiccounsel.com/our_news/polls/
    Canada-USA%20Poll%20-%20final2%20-%20posted2.
    pdf] (accessed January 21, 2009).

9   "The State of the News Media 2006," Project for Excellence
    in Journalism, [http://www.stateofthenewsmedia.
    org/2006/] (accessed January 21, 2009).

10 The Project for Excellence in Journalism's annual report
    on the news media noted that in 2006, Fox News' median
    prime-time audience dropped 14 percent and its median
    daytime viewership fell by 12 percent. "The State of the
    News Media 2007," Project for Excellence in Journalism,
    http://www.stateofthenewsmedia.org/2007/ (accessed
    January 21, 2009).

11 "The State of the News Media 2008," Project for Excellence
    in Journalism, [http://www.stateofthenewsmedia.
    org/2008/] (accessed January 22, 2009).

12 Ibid.

13 Doug Struck, "Canada Fights Myth it was 9/11 Conduit;
    Charge Often Repeated by U.S. Officials," Washington Post,
    April 9, 2005, A20. Also: Bob Drogin, "Not so quiet on
    the northern front," Los Angeles Times, May 10, 2009, A3.

14 Ibid.

15 For further reference — Neil Henry, American Carnival;
    Journalism Under Siege in an Age of New Media, (Berkeley:
    University of California Press, 2007), 189-191. Also:
    Eric Rothenbuhler, "Frank N. Magid Associates," The
    Museum of Broadcast Communications, [http://www.
    museum.tv/archives/etv/M/htmlM/magidfrank/
    magidfrank.html] (accessed January 23, 2009).

16   "The Web: Alarming, Appealing and a Challenge to
      Journalistic Values," The Pew Research Center for the
      People & the Press, March 17, 2008, [http://www.
      stateofthenewsmedia.com/2008/Journalist%20report%2
      02008.pdf] (accessed May 30, 2008)
17   Chris Kelly, comment on "The National Review Invades
      Canada," Huffington Post Blog, comment posted August 3,
      2007, [http://www.huffingtonpost.com/chris-kelly/the-
      national-reviewi_b_59058.html] (accessed May 30, 2007).
18   Ibid.
19   Bob Drogin and Mark Z. Barabak, "McCain says Obama
      wants socialism," Los Angeles Times, October 19, 2008,
      A20.
20   Barack Obama's campaign team certainly seemed aware
      of how the comments could be perceived in Canada. In
      February and March 2008, the American and Canadian
      media widely circulated news of a leaked Canadian
      government memo that mentioned how an Obama
      campaign staffer assured Canadian diplomats that the
      criticisms against NAFTA were more campaign rhetoric
      than a potential shift in policy.
21   The State of the News Media 2007 report also theorized
      that Fox could be losing viewers to rival cable networks
      or other forms of media, perhaps as a result of its shows
      becoming too familiar and a loss of audience interest.
      For reference: "The State of the News Media 2007,"
      Project for Excellence in Journalism, [http://www.
      stateofthenewsmedia.org/2007/] (accessed January
      24, 2009). Also, "The State of the News Media 2008,"
      Project for Excellence in Journalism, [http://www.
      stateofthenewsmedia.org/2008/] (accessed
      January 24, 2009).
22   CBC Arts, "Canadian Correspondents a Rare Breed for
      U.S. Newspapers," cbcnews.ca, April 4, 2007, [http://
      www.cbc.ca/arts/media/story/2007/04/04/canadian-
      correspondents.html] (accessed May 31, 2008).

★★★ BIBLIOGRAPHY ★★★

Individual entries for newspaper stories from the *New York Times, Chicago Tribune, Washington Post, Los Angeles Times, Wall Street Journal, Christian Science Monitor,* and *Washington Times* are contained in the footnotes.

Campbell, Alex. "Canada's Future." *New Republic,* March 9, 1968.

Canadian Broadcasting Corporation. "Canadian Correspondents a Rare Breed for U.S. Newspapers." April 4, 2007. http://www.cbc.ca/arts/media/story/2007/04/04/ canadian-correspondents.html.

———. "Anti-Bush protesters scuffle with police." December 1, 2004, http://www.cbc.ca/canada/story/2004/11/30/ bush_arrives041130.html.

———. "Draft-Dodger Memorial to be Built in B.C." September 8, 2004, http://www.cbc.ca/story/canada/national/2004/09/08/draft_dogers040908.html.

———. "Martin rejects U.S. ambassador's rebuke." December 13, 2005, http://www.cbc.ca/story/canadavotes2006/national/2005/12/13/wilkins-051213.html.

———. "Timeline of BSE in Canada and the U.S." October 23, 2006, http://www.cbc.ca/news/background/madcow/timeline.html.

Carlson, Tucker. "Security Shakeup" (Transcript). CNN *Crossfire,* November 30, 2004. http://transcripts.cnn.com/TRANSCRIPTS/0411/30/cf.01.html.

Clements, Kendrick A. "Manifest Destiny and Canadian Reciprocity in 1911." *The Pacific Historical Review* 42, no. 1 (February 1973): 32–52.

Cooper, Charles A. "Trading with the Communists." *New Republic,* October 12, 1963.

Deane, Philip. "Canada–US: Inevitable Allies." *New Republic,* April 29, 1957.

Embassy of Canada, Washington. "The Canada–U.S. Trade
    and Investment Partnership." http://geo.international.
    gc.ca/can-am/. washington/trade_and_investment/
    trade_partnership-en.asp.
Foreign Affairs and International Trade Canada. "Canada's
    Actions Against Terrorism Since September 11." http://
    www.dfait-maeci.gc.ca/anti-terrorism/Canadaactions-en.asp.
——. "Natural Gas." http://geo.international.gc.ca/can-am/
    main/right_nav/natural_gas-en.asp.
——. "Oil." http://geo.international.gc.ca/can-am/main/
    right_nav/oil-en.asp.
Gibson, John. "Un-Happy Birthday, Canada." *Maclean's*,
    July 1, 2005.
Goldberg, Jonah. "Bomb Canada: The Case for War."
    National Review, November 25, 2002.
——. "Soviet Canuckistan." *National Review Online*,
    November 8, 2002.
Ipsos-Reid. "Seven-in-Ten (72%) Canadians Support U.S.
    Led Air Strikes on Terrorist Targets in Afghanistan."
    October 15, 2001.
Labash, Matt. "Welcome to Canada: The Great White Waste
    of Time." *Weekly Standard* 10.25, March 21, 2005.
Media Matters for America. "Blame Canada! Cavuto:
    '[H]ave the Canadians gotten a little too big for their
    britches?'" December 16, 2005. http://mediamatters.
    org/items/200512160008.
——. "Canada in the crosshairs: Media conservatives sling
    mud north of the border." December 16, 2005. http://
    mediamatters.org/items/200512160012.
——. "Coulter: Canada is 'lucky we allow them to exist on
    the same continent'; Carlson: 'Without the U.S., Canada
    is essentially Honduras'" November 30, 2004. http://
    mediamatters.org/items/200412010011.
——. "O'Reilly: 'They've got all kinds of Muslim crazies up in
    Canada running around.'" February 24, 2006. http://
    mediamatters.org/items/200602240004.
Michaels, Guy, and Xiaojia Zhi. "Freedom Fries." CEP
    Discussion Paper No 815. London School of Economics
    and Political Science, July 2007.

Owen, David. "Penny Dreadful." *The New Yorker*, March 31, 2008.

Pew Research Center for the People and the Press. "Americans and Canadians: The North American Not-so-Odd Couple." http://people-press.org/commentary/?analysisid=80.

———. "The Web: Alarming, Appealing and a Challenge to Journalistic Values." http://www.stateofthenewsmedia. com/2008/Journalist%20report%202008.pdf.

Project for Excellence in Journalism. "The State of the News Media 2006." http://www.stateofthenewsmedia. org/2006/.

———. "The State of the News Media 2007." http://www. stateofthenewsmedia.org/2007/.

———. "The State of the News Media 2008." http://www. stateofthenewsmedia.org/2008/.

Rothenbuhler, Eric. "Frank N. Magid Associates." The Museum of Broadcast Communications, http://www. museum.tv/archives/etv/M/htmlM/magidfrank/ magidfrank.htm.

Saad, Lydia. "China Down, France up in Americans' Ratings." Gallup, March 3, 2008. http://www.gallup.com/ poll/104719/China-Down-France-Americans-Ratings. aspx.

Strategic Counsel. "Canadians' Perceptions and Attitudes Towards the United States." March 27, 2006. http:// www.thestrategiccounsel.com/our_news/polls/ 2006-03-27%20GMCTV%20Mar25-26%20(Mar27).pdf.

———. "A Tale of Two Nations; State of Canadian/ American Public Opinion." June 2008. http://www. thestrategiccounsel.com/our_news/polls/Canada-USA%20Poll%20-%20final2%20-%20posted2.pdf.

Thompson, John Herd, and Mark Paul Richard. "Canadian History in North American Context." In *Canadian Studies in the New Millennium*, edited by Patrick James and Mark Kasoff, 37–64. Toronto: University of Toronto Press, 2008.

For further reading on Canada–US relations, as well as the American media, please refer to the following books.

Adams, Michael. *Fire and Ice: The United States, Canada and the Myth of Converging Values*. Toronto: Penguin Canada, 2003.

Doran, Charles F. *Why Canadian Unity Matters and Why Americans Care: Democratic Pluralism at Risk*. Toronto: University of Toronto Press, 2001.

Downie Jr., Leonard, and Robert G. Kaiser. *The News About the News: American Journalism in Peril*. New York: Vintage Books, 2003.

Granatstein, J.L., and Norman Hillmer. *For Better or for Worse: Canada and the United States to the 1990s*. Mississauga, ON: Copp Clark Pitman, 1991.

Harrison, Trevor W. "Anti-Canadianism: Explaining the Deep Roots of a Shallow Phenomenon." *International Journal of Canadian Studies*, no. 35 (2007): 217-239.

Henry, Neil. *American Carnival: Journalism Under Siege in an Age of New Media*. Berkeley: University of California Press, 2007.

MacDonald, David. "Anti-Americanism and Anti-Canadianism: A New Look at Canada–US Relations." Paper presented at the annual meeting for the International Studies Association, San Francisco. March 26, 2008.

Orchard, David. *The Fight for Canada: Four Centuries of Resistance to American Expansionism*. Westmount, QC: Robert Davies Multimedia, 1998.

Thompson, John Herd, and Stephen J. Randall. *Canada and the United States: Ambivalent Allies*. 4th ed. Athens, GA: University of Georgia Press, 2008.

Illustration Sources

Page 4 In the public domain.

Page 7 In the public domain.

Page 16 Courtesy of the "Ding" Darling Wildlife Society.

Page 24 In the public domain.

Page 29 In the public domain.

Page 30 In the public domain.

Page 38 From *The Washington Post*, 22 February © 1959 *The Washington Post*. All rights reserved. Used by permission and protected by the Copyright Laws of the United States. The printing, copying, redistribution, or retransmission of the Material without express written permission is prohibited.

Page 47 From *Chicago Tribune*, 12 February © 1965 *Chicago Tribune*. All rights reserved. Used by permission and protected by the Copyright Laws of the United States. The printing, copying, redistribution, or retransmission of the Material without express written permission is prohibited.

Page 51 From *Chicago Tribune*, 3 March © 1967 *Chicago Tribune*. All rights reserved. Used by permission and protected by the Copyright Laws of the United States. The printing, copying, redistribution, or retransmission of the Material without express written permission is prohibited.

Page 63 Courtesy of the *Dayton Daily News*.

Page 64 From *Chicago Tribune*, 28 December © 1973 *Chicago Tribune*. All rights reserved. Used by permission and protected by the Copyright Laws of the United States. The printing, copying, redistribution, or retransmission of the Material without express written permission is prohibited.

Page 65 Courtesy of the *Winnipeg Free Press*.

Page 69 Courtesy of United Press International.

Page 78 Copyright © 2001 *The New Yorker Collection* from cartoonbank.com. All Rights Reserved.

Page 85 Copyright © 2002 by National Review, Inc., 215 Lexington Avenue, New York, NY 10016. Reprinted by permission.

Page 94 Courtesy of Media Matters for America.

★★★ INDEX ★★★

Photography by Zarek

Chantal Allan is an award-winning journalist who has reported for CBC Radio and NPR (National Public Radio). Her articles have appeared in the *Toronto Star* and the *Los Angeles Daily News*, among other publications. She received her M.A. in journalism from the University of Southern California and lives in Los Angeles.

This book was set in Goudy Old Style.